"CALL ME JOHN"

A Life of Pope John XXIII

BY

RICHARD CARDINAL CUSHING

UT COGNOSCANT TE

ST. PAUL EDITIONS

Library of Congress Catalog Card Number: 63-22752

Copyright, 1963, by the *Daughters of St. Paul*

Printed by the *Daughters of St. Paul*
50 St. Paul's Ave., Jamaica Plain, Boston, Mass. 02130

CONTENTS

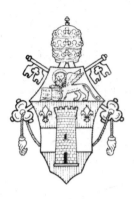

"EVERYBODY CALLS ME JOHN!"

Above her crib at Gesu Bambino Hospital in Rome, the ceiling was white and lonely for six-year-old Maria.

Lying there with her spine in a sheath-like plaster cast, she played a lonesome role. Her loneliness was broken only by occasional visits from her parents, by trays of food. Then, of course, there were the periodic activities of the Sister-nurse and the Doctor who were trying very hard to make Maria's back grow straight and strong.

Looking at the desert vacancy of the ceiling now, in mid-morning, Maria wondered when its total emptiness would be filled by the pleasant face of a very important and famous man.

Sister had told Maria, early that morning, that there was a very good chance the ward would be visited by an elderly priest who happened to be the Pastor of the Catholic Church, all over the world.

"He walks in and out of the hospital just like the chaplain!" she exclaimed, widening her eyes and shrugging her shoulders with sheer delight.

Sister then gave Maria a colored photograph of this kindly holy man who had a title like "papa" and whose printed name, at the bottom of the photo read: Pontifex Maximus, Pope John XXIII.

"He is the Pope, the head priest of the Catholic Church, and he just might come to see you this morning," said Sister, while taking Maria's temperature.

"Now what do you think of that?" the nun asked cheerily, popping the thermometer out of Maria's lips and cocking a merry eye at what it had to tell her.

"Pope? That sounds like 'Papa'," Maria said.

"Yes, like Papa," Sister said. "He is very real and gentle. You will be able to talk with him like your own papa. Ask him to write something for you on his picture, if you like."

"Yes, yes," Maria said, smiling broadly, much taken with the idea.

Again, the lonely whiteness of the ceiling. An hour, two hours, three, went by. Now, new people in the ward. A feeling of excitement, electricity, yes, tickles along her spine, under the grim grip of the plaster cast. He must be here, Pope, Papa, head priest of all the world. What shall I call him? Big man, good man, holy man . . . .

The excitement moved slowly toward her, pausing, it seemed, for quite long periods at the beds of the other children on both sides of the aisle.

Maria heard Sister introducing him to each child. She heard his gentle, jolly voice; it was jolly like . . . like Santa Claus. She heard the rich, subdued laughter which had a way of making Maria want to laugh; she heard the prayers, too, the deep-throated blessings as the 'excitement' moved closer.

"Maria, this is the Holy Father. Of all the little girls, he especially wanted to meet you." Thus she was introduced to the most loved pope of all times.

The lonely whiteness of the ceiling was gone. In its place, a great, kind face. He wore a white skull cap and looked on her with such kindness and concern that he might have been her real 'papa'.

"Maria, how are you, my dear child?" he asked, taking her little, toy hand lightly in his strong, gentle hand that years ago became large and powerful while working on the farm that supported his family.

"I am fine, . . ." Maria strove for words, nervous, anxious, somewhat overwhelmed. "I am fine, Papa, I mean, Holy Father. . . ."

She was confused as to what to call the Pope and he sensed this immediately.

"Everybody calls me John," the Pope said, making a jest out of a commonplace truth. "Won't you call me John, too, Maria?"

"Yes, yes, John," Maria said.

UNDER THE MOUNTAIN

Everybody calls him John now, it is true; Pope John to be more exact; Good Pope John, if we're going to be warm-hearted about his memory. And it is almost impossible to speak or think about the late Pope John without being warm-hearted.

Yet there was a time when he lived in the Italian farm village that is called Sotte il Monte (Under The Mountain), when everybody called him Angelo.

Angelo Giuseppe Roncalli was born on November 25, 1881, and he could not have known that the French troops had just invaded the Italian colony at Tunis and caused the fall of the current Italian government.

He was born amid change and intended for changing times.

Later in his life–after World War II, to be exact–when Cardinal-Diplomat, or Papal Nuncio to Paris, Angelo Roncalli would charm and reason the French into an era of good feeling toward the Vatican and all of Italy.

When Angelo was only a year old, and before he was large enough to climb the hill called Colle San Giovanni–under which his village was built–the great patriot Garibaldi, who had inflamed all of Italy with new ideas and actions, passed away.

Garibaldi had a particular interest in Angelo's home area. It was from the neighboring big city of Bergamo that this exciting leader had recruited many of his fierce, brave troops known as "Bergamese".

Even with some of his anti-clerical tendencies, Garibaldi was aware of the fact that the countrymen of Angelo Roncalli were hard and strong in two kinds of patriotism: loyalty to the Pope and loyalty to Italy. The Bergamese deeply believed that one kind of loyalty was indivisible from the other.

As the third oldest of thirteen children (three of whom died young), the toddling child, Angelo, soon learned at the knees of his mother, Maria Anna, and in the gnarled grip of his father, Giovanni Battista, that God and country go together as naturally as spaghetti and red wine.

In the years of childhood, Angelo played in the sun-filled dooryard with his brothers and sisters. Above the door of the three-story stone building he could see the family motto inscribed in Latin: "Obedientia et Pax."

Peace and obedience, these he knew as a child, even as he was to know them as a farm worker, a seminarian, a priest, a Pope of all the world.

In the heat of the day, Angelo took refuge with his family among the grape vines. He saw the grape, the rice, the corn in all its changes. He learned the cycle of tilling the soil from the time of the melting snows in the mountain springtime, through the long, hot summer and into the harvest amid the soft, cool mists of autumn.

The corn meal was in their staple dish, polenta, mixed with chopped meat, baked in a loaf and then sliced to be eaten, hot or cold. The grape was in the wine which all drank with meals. The wheat that waved in a haze of gold on the mountainside was eventually in the ravioli and macaroni.

"Angelo, Angelo!" he heard his mother calling, late in the summer, as his sixth birthday approached. The lean, red mongrel barked wildly, heralding activity from over the hill.

Angelo dashed from the cow barn where he had helped his brother Alfredo settle the great, mild beasts for the night. They were coming! They were coming from Bergamo, bringing his new school shoes.

In his tough, bare feet he sprinted over the stony path to meet his parents. A hug, a kiss, the shoes were his to unwrap, to stroke, to wear.

That night, around the open fire, the Roncallis listened to a reading by Uncle Zaverio who intoned the glories of Roman history, the biblical excitement of

David and Goliath and some snippets of modern thought from a fashionable Spanish author.

In a shadowy corner, Angelo wiggled his toes in a pair of shoes for the very first time.

Uncle Zaverio squinted through the firelight at the printed words and spoke out the wisdom and lusty adventures of Julius Caesar, Saul of Tarsus, Constantine the Great.

Tomorrow, Angelo would go to Sunday Mass in his shoes with his older brothers. Tomorrow, too, he would attend Catechism class for the first time.

Soon came September, and he was off to the neighboring village of Carvico where he would be taught the three R's by the parish priest. The three R's were to be accompanied by the big L of Latin, a preparation for more formal schooling when he would have reached the age of nine.

Beyond the crest of the hill, after waving goodbye to his parents, Angelo sat on a rock and waited for his neighbor, Pietro Donizetto, who would accompany him to school.

His blood was quickened by the impact of the wild, wonderful new world opening up before him. In an isolated pine tree, stark against the mountain peak of Monte Canto, a crow cawed out a warning of Angelo's presence to several black brethren circling high above him.

"Look out below! Look out below!" the crow seemed to be screaming, almost with the clarity of human speech.

Angelo sat on the flat rock in the mild, sweet sun of early morning, wondering at the intelligence of crows.

From this luxury of thought he shifted to the luxury of waggling his toes in his strong, black, high-top shoes.

"If I walked in my bare feet, I would not disturb the crows," he thought. "But more importantly I would save the leather of my shoes."

He unlaced his shoes, removed them, took off his thick, homespun socks, stuffed them separately into his shoes, then tied the shoes together with their tough leather thongs.

The cawing of the crows, which had been stilled for a while, started up in panic again. The crunching of stone from the eastern slope of the hill signaled Pietro's approach.

"Ha, Angelo," Pietro called in mockery, "you have taken off your shoes already. Do they hurt you so?"

"No, signor," Angelo said, rising with the shoes draped snugly around his neck and shoulders. "I will make them last longer this way. I will walk on the grass beside the stony path. Don't you want to do it, too? Take off your shoes. We shall do this together."

Pietro slackened his jaw, struck with the idea. Then he sat down on the same flat stone and duplicated the actions of Angelo, even to the arrangement of the shoes about his neck and shoulders.

While he was doing this, Angelo looked at the towering but climbable height of Monte Canto.

"Uncle Zaverio you told me you can see the Cathedral of Milan from up there on a clear day," Angelo reflected.

"Faugh!" Pietro snorted. "Is it possible?"

"If Uncle Zaverio says it is possible, it is possible," Angelo answered. "I would like to climb that mountain some clear morning when we do not have to go to school. Will you go with me?"

"Yes, paisan," Pietro said with a touch of scorn, "this I would like to see."

"We will do it. Come with me now to school, Pietro. You know, you could be nicknamed doubting Thomas," Angelo said.

They moved briskly down the hill toward Carvico in their bare feet. Two pair of shoes knocked gently against two sturdy young chests as they walked on opposite sides of the path where the grassy sward cushioned the lightness of their steps.

When Angelo was nine years old, in 1890, Pope Leo XIII had denounced Italy's King Humbert as a usurper. Pope Leo was locked in a bitter struggle with the anti-clericals who advocated complete destruction of the temporal rights of the Papacy.

Angelo, now a student at the high school of the Episcopal College at Celano, still walked to school in his bare feet, whenever he could, and still accompanied by his friend Pietro.

If Pope Leo was struggling with the anti-clericals, his future successor, Angelo Roncalli, had his own struggles with books. The farm and the family were uppermost in Angelo's mind, even in high school, and his grades were mediocre at best.

On the way home from school he often stopped to visit with his aunt, a housekeeper in the rectory of Don Martinelli, parish priest of San Gregorio. Here, his aunt fed him as he warmed himself by the kitchen stove in the chill of winter and early spring.

It was to Don Martinelli that his teacher addressed a note concerning Angelo's sagging scholastic standing at Celano.

Angelo did not know the contents of the sealed letter to Don Martinelli, but it did not take much imagination to figure out just what it contained.

That afternoon, Angelo again soaked up the heat by the rectory's kitchen stove as his aunt fed him a hot slice of polenta.

They discussed many things: their family, the farm, the latest Spanish author whom Uncle Zaverio was reading. Angelo came, he rested, he supped, he went on home.

Yet, in some ancient schoolboy tradition, the letter of reproach from his teacher to Don Martinelli was never delivered—from that day to this.

When he was eleven years old, Angelo went to school in a cassock and Roman collar even though he was not actually studying to become a priest.

In his time and place, if you went on to higher education, it simply meant you went to the Seminary in Bergamo where the only competent, organized teachers were available.

Angelo's religious faith was deep and strong, like that of his entire family and the people of the whole Bergamo area. On the surface, at least, he did not seem to be struck by any vocation to the priesthood. He seemed to grow into his vocation gradually, even as he grew slowly into scholarly pursuits as a student.

At Bergamo, in 1891, Angelo had his first picture taken. It was a somewhat expensive undertaking, made possible only by the gift of a benefactor who remains nameless. Back home on the farm, only five miles over the mountains, there were few if any family photographs, simply because there was no money available for such luxuries.

In three-score years Angelo was to become the most photographed man in the world.

He had come to Bergamo when it was a mighty fortress of Catholicism in strife-torn Italy. Pope Leo was beset by the anti-clerical agitators of the awakening democracy. But he had the bulwark of Bergamo. He had all its united depth of faith and patriotism to give the Vatican the aid and comfort in scholarship and priest-power which it so desperately needed.

Providential is the word for the growing-space and shelter which a future Pope knew at the minor seminary. He lived in peace while the Pope, Leo XIII, held the line for Christian freedom against the enemies of the Church.

Now came the true flowering of the basically good mind of Angelo Roncalli. Previously his thoughts had been engaged with the menial things of the farm and the binding but wholesome involvements of family life. Angelo now turned to history and theology, more brilliant in his skill at research than in the drudgery of rote learning.

Among writers he turned to the novelist Manzoni who placed the setting of his famed romance "The Betrothed" in and around Angelo's home country. Manzoni completely understood Christian love in all its phases: boy meets girl, man and wife, father and mother.

Angelo had known all this in the farming family community and he was attracted to Manzoni because of his deep understanding of Christian love.

The world of music opened up to the awakened Roncalli. It had in its newness a more wondrous attraction than the simple folk tunes of his childhood. The delicacy of Mozart, the solemnity of Bach, he came to know and love. He preferred the more tasteful Donizetti in operetta over the extremely popular Verdi.

At fourteen he took the "tonsure," the cutting of the hair of a seminarian which symbolized the crowning with thorns and which was an open indication of the seriousness of one's vocation.

Don Martinelli would have been impressed by Angelo's proficiency in Latin, Greek, Italian and world history, mathematics, geometry, physics, chemistry, the Italian language and world literature.

"Put out the lights, Mr. Prefect, I'm in bed. . . ."

Even as Percy Wynn called out that compliance in the pages of boys' books a decade ago, so, too, did Bergamese seminarians call out to their newly appointed dormitory prefect, Angelo Roncalli in 1895.

Five years later, in 1900, having completed his pre-college training, Angelo was sent by his perceptive superiors to the Seminario Romano, following in the footsteps of two other mountain men who were to become Pope before him: Giuseppe Sarto (Pius X) and Achille Ratti (Pius XI).

Angelo was surely "destiny's tot"–which he was often to be in his lifetime–arriving in Rome, as he did, at the beginning of the Holy Year proclaimed by ninety-year-old Pope Leo XIII.

Leo, standing up valiantly, like an old oak against die-hard anti-clericals, knew he had the majority of the Italians with him. In addition, he flooded the Eternal

City with distinguished clergy and laity from all over the world.

Amid all this carnival and all this reverent ceremony of the Holy Year, Angelo Roncalli, the simple farm boy, arrived in Rome.

Canon law and history soon absorbed him. It was typical of his own gift for wit and humor that he should become a devoted follower of that saintly humorist, St. Philip Neri, who had in the 16th century reformed the religious and secular life of Rome.

This appealed to something vital and lasting in Angelo. This achievement of Neri's life stirred the something in Angelo that was later to prompt similar, yet world-wide reforms on the part of the future Pope John.

In late October of 1901 Angelo sat in the library at the Seminary, deeply absorbed in the *Annales Ecclesiastici*, a famous historical work of Cesare Cardinal Baronio who was a contemporary and admirer of St. Philip Neri.

Although deeply absorbed, Angelo sensed the approach of footsteps. Looking up slowly, he beheld Father Rector blinking somewhat owlishly at him through his metal rimmed spectacles.

"Angelo, I have what may seem to be bad news for you."

"The Virgin sustain us, Father Rector! Is it my mother, papa, someone is ill?"

"No, no, son," Father Rector said. "Nothing like that. You've been called into military service. You can volunteer for a year, if you like, with choice of branch. If you let the grace period expire, you'll be drafted for a longer period of time."

Angelo panicked for just a moment. He thought about his good life at the seminary, with the priesthood almost in his grasp. But only one year, just one year, if he volunteered.

"I'll volunteer, Father Rector, with your permission, right away. I'll volunteer for the infantry!"

Angelo paused, recovering from the shock of his sudden decision.

The real, true Angelo Roncalli of ever-present wit and humor again took possession of his being. "After all, Father Rector," he said with an impish smile, "who's better suited for hiking with the infantry? I've been climbing over mountains all my life!"

SOLDIER AND SECRETARY

"Left, right! Left, right! Brigade HALT!"

In the dusty quadrangle outside the barracks of the 73rd Infantry Regiment of the Italian Army, the Lombardy Brigade stood at attention.

It was early June, 1902. These "draftees", grimy with sweat and dust, straining under full packs and heavy rifles, had just finished a "forced march."

They had trudged back and forth to a distant camp in the mountains, bringing to a climax their sixth month of rigorous army training.

No longer soft and green citizen soldiers, they stood firmly at attention. Among them, in the rear rank, stood Private Angelo Roncalli, a former seminarian. He tightened his jaw muscles to keep himself from crying out with sheer exhaustion.

Before them, a scowling, dust-laden Captain stood in careful scrutiny of his men.

Several moments passed. Silence. Tension. A desperate refusal on the part of all to buckle or cry out.

Finally, the stern, machine-like Captain spoke.

"Now, you are beginning to be soldiers of the Italian Army," he said.

Private Roncalli felt the tickly rivulets of sweat rolling down his face, down under his soggy shirt, fanning out in prickly sorties along his chest and shoulders.

"You are still at attention for a good reason," the Captain continued. "Even though your legs are ready to fall from under you, you must follow orders. A soldier must learn to stand even without legs!"

"You have borne yourselves like soldiers!" the Captain said, his hard, ruddy face, softening with a hint of affection. "My compliments to you. BRIGADE DISMISSED!"

Down with the rifles, off with the searing straps of the full packs. Sighs. Moans of relief. Many slumped down to the ground, untying their bootstraps, pulling off their ponderous shoes.

Many simply sunk to a seat on their packs and groaned with sheer relief.

Private Angelo Roncalli sat on his pack, removed his cap and towelled the perspiration from his face and neck with a large kerchief.

Beside him, slim, delicate Private Biagi rubbed his raw shoulders, sobbing with complete fatigue.

"Come, Luigi," Angelo said tenderly, "a good, hot shower, soap and water, a rubdown with cool ointment. You will feel much better. And then—sleep, sleep, as much as you want. We do not answer Reveille tomorrow."

The two privates arose slowly. Luigi wobbled at the knees.

"Come, Luigi, I will carry your pack." Angelo said.

Luigi smiled with gratitude.

"Thank you, Angelo, I will carry the rifles."

Private Roncalli, with one last huge effort, gripped the straps of both packs and swung their weights along on either side of him. Slowly, steadily, he followed Luigi into the barracks.

Now that the ordeal of the forced march was ended, many of the "buck" privates with six months service were eligible for promotion to Corporal. One of these was Angelo Roncalli.

This was his first big step up the ladder in military life. In the army he would later advance to Sergeant and Chaplain-Lieutenant. In religion he would eventually become "Commander-in-Chief" of all the "armies" of the Catholic Faith.

Years later, Pope John modestly recalled his two promotions to non-commissioned officer. In the American army we call corporals and sergeants: "NCO's". Thus, Angelo became an N.C.O.

"I was promoted to Corporal," said good Pope John, "merely because one who has normal health and intelligence must become a corporal after six months."

This is similar to the familiar joke about American army draftees. About them it is humorously said that if the examining doctor can detect a heart-beat, they shall be pronounced I-A, fit and ready for duty.

Pope John, in continued reminiscence to a group of Italian war veterans, tells us about his promotion to, and experiences as, a Sergeant.

"After a time, I was a candidate for promotion to the rank of Sergeant."

He took an examination for this promotion but, in his own words: "It went just so-so."

"They asked me to give the order for a platoon to attack," the Pope recalled. "I, who had never yet given the command to stand at attention!"

Sometimes 'Sergeant Roncalli' had to give out company punishment to his men. But he never burdened them with anything heavier than confinement to barracks.

One sunny day he came across a soldier who was sitting glumly on his bunk, staring at the barracks wall.

"Why aren't you outside taking recreation with the others?" Sergeant Roncalli asked.

"You confined me to barracks," was the answer.

"I confined you to barracks only for the night. It is daylight. Now you can go out," the Sergeant said, smiling.

When Angelo completed his year of military service, he returned to his studies for the priesthood in Rome.

He was in the Eternal City when Pope Leo XIII died in 1903. Several days later, he saw the white smoke waft up from the rickety stove pipe of the Sistine Chapel. This signified the election of Giuseppe Sarto as Pope Pius X.

White smoke over the Vatican has for many decades signified the moment of election of our Popes.

It is said that if Pius X had not changed his mind, at one point, Angelo Roncalli might never have become Pope John XXIII.

The report goes this way: When Pope Pius X was Cardinal Sarto, he was asked what name he would choose if ever he became Pope.

"If it happens, I can tell you I will call myself John XXIII," Cardinal Sarto answered.

But he changed his mind apparently, and the name of John XXIII was left available to Angelo Roncalli in a later day of triumph.

Soon arrived what was probably the happiest day in Angelo's life. On August 10, 1904, he was ordained to the priesthood at the Church of Santa Maria in Monte Santo, a suburb of Rome. On the following day, the brand new Father Roncalli celebrated his first mass in St. Peter's Basilica.

What must have been the thoughts of this future Pontiff as he read the Mass at an altar next to the tomb of St. Peter, the first of all Popes.

Angelo was a priest forever! He had worn a cassock since he was eleven years old at the Seminary High School in Bergamo.

He said his Mass above the sainted bones of the man upon whom Christ had built his Church. "Thou art Peter. . . ."

He could not have known that he, Angelo Roncalli, would one day be the remote successor of St. Peter.

At that first Mass the heart of Father Roncalli turned to the simple, peasant folk at home, "Under The Mountain." It was there, barefooted, with his shoes slung over his shoulders, that he had taken his first steps toward the priesthood.

And, there, he returned, on August 15, 1904, to offer his "other" first Mass for his family and his friends.

On that Feast of the Assumption we can be sure that Father Roncalli preached to his loved ones, his friends and neighbors, the similar thoughts about his priesthood which he was one day to express as Archbishop of Venice:

"Ever since I was born I have had no thought of becoming anything other than a priest. A priest is supposed to comfort and enlighten souls and he is able to fulfill his mission because he himself feels the weight of human frailty. His task is, above all, to dispense grace, to administer the Sacraments."

Father Roncalli remained in and around Bergamo until the outbreak of World War I and for a time thereafter.

The new Bishop of Bergamo, Giacomo Radini-Tedeschi, was in need of a secretary. Father Roncalli, who had assisted at the consecration ceremonies of the new Bishop in Rome, was recommended for the job. He was actually recommended for the post by another young cleric who had refused the position.

This was surely the up-turning point of Father Roncalli's career as a future luminary in church affairs.

Bishop Radini was already famed all over Italy as Minister of Propaganda under the late Pope Leo XIII. He had been what we call in America, a public relations man and publicity director for the Vatican.

You can imagine the guidance and friendships his secretary might benefit by when you consider that Bishop Radini was a close friend and aide of Pope Pius X, as well as a friend and associate of two future Popes: Pope Benedict XV and Pope Pius XI.

The latter two were then Monsignor Della Chiesa and Monsignor Achille Ratti, respectively.

Bishop Radini, in the light of history, was now to add another future Pope to his intimate circle.

Radini was in charge of all Italian pilgrimages to various holy shrines throughout Europe. This required extensive travel at certain times of the year.

These holy and colorful journeys almost always included his secretary, Father Angelo. The latter thus became familiar with the great Marian shrine of Lourdes in France. He walked the path of St. John Vianney in the famous French country town of Ars. Angelo knelt with his Bishop and groups of Italian pilgrims at Paray-le-Monial where St. Margaret Mary Alacoque beheld the vision of the Sacred Heart.

Parallel with these visits, Father Angelo met the great and the powerful of the civil and clerical world. Bishop Radini was renowned as a social reformer and wherever he went, men of grandeur sought out his advice and attention.

Thus, Father Angelo, through these personal contacts, arranged by the Bishop, was literally going to prep school as a future international diplomat.

Along with his secretarial duties, this energetic "new curate" served as teacher of Church History at the Seminary in Bergamo.

In connection with this field of work, Bishop Radini wanted Father Angelo to meet and know his friend, Monsignor Achille Ratti. Ratti was famed, even then, as a fearless mountain climber and conqueror of the Alps. He was, of course, to become even more famous as Pope Pius XI.

The trip to Monsignor Ratti's library in Milan concerned an essay on the tolerant and sunny St. Charles Borromeo.

"We should do something about our mutual admiration for St. Charles," Bishop Radini suggested to Angelo. "Specifically, I suggest you write about St. Charles who spent many days and nights right here in the Bergamo area."

There was a mischievous twinkle in the wise old Bishop's eyes. He wanted Angelo to meet Achille Ratti for future as well as present reasons.

"You must study certain documents at the Ambrosian library in Milan. They will tell you about the city and the times in which St. Charles lived. It will strongly supplement the material we have here about his days in Bergamo. I will give you a letter to the librarian, Monsignor Ratti. He will help you."

Then Father Angelo travelled to Milan to do the research and also meet the future Pope.

"Dignified, cordial, his broad and open-browed head inclined toward me while he listened"—These were Angelo's reactions to Achille Ratti.

Monsignor Ratti heard the young priest's plan of research and then asked him to return in a few days.

During that time he personally went through the dusty archives and found the volumes Father Angelo had requested.

The future Pope, twenty-five years older than Angelo, made photostatic copies of the volumes so that the young scholar could take all the material back to Bergamo.

Bishop Radini's enthusiasm for the project later brought forth a humorous observation from his secretary who was one day to be famed for his ready wit in the Vatican chambers.

The Bishop formed several committees to help Father Angelo with the final work of research on the book about St. Charles.

There was a great to-do, including public statements, pledges of funds, enlarged sub-committees.

When the work was done, Father Angelo, in a preface to the work, made the following observation:

"But as often happens, so it happened in this case too: a project begins with the naming of committees, but the work has to be done by one single person."

What Father Angelo said, with a touch of mischief but no malice, could be put this way in American parlance: "If you want anything done right, do it yourself."

A sense of wonder would soon surround the deaths of two friends who were known and loved by Father Angelo.

Just before the First World War was to sweep like a grassfire across all of Europe, the saintly Pope Pius X passed away.

Two days later, the Pope's good friend, Bishop Radini, died in the strong and loving arms of his clerical secretary.

The Bishop was too weak to pray. Father Roncalli provided the lips and the voice.

"O Jesus crucified, forgive my sins. . . ." the young secretary prayed, as the life of a great Italian Bishop ebbed away.

Even amid his deep sadness, Father Roncalli knew the wonderment of a story Bishop Radini had told him.

The Bishop and Pius X were so close that Pius promised to come and get Radini and personally escort him to Heaven, should the Pope die first.

"Pius X came for the Bishop in just two days." Father Angelo knew. "They are in heaven together."

A new Pope and a new war.

Pope Benedict XV took over the helm of Peter's great boat as the bugles blew and the war drums rolled across the continent and in many far corners of the globe.

Father Roncalli was immediately called back into service as a Sergeant and was assigned to a military hospital as a medical aide.

The healer of souls was now a healer of bodies as well.

All the Roncalli brothers were mustered into service at once. Mother Roncalli endured many restless nights in watchful prayer, thinking of her sons under fire. She thought particularly of one whose heart ached for his beloved work of teaching at the seminary of Bergamo.

During this period, Sergeant Roncalli grew a moustache. Legend tells us he permitted the "growth" to make his young face seem more mature. He was always the priest, even as a medic, and it would appear that in counseling and comforting soldiers wounded on the Austrian front, he wanted to seem to be more of a "grizzled" veteran.

In 1916 it was decreed that all priests in the service would become chaplains with the rank of lieutenant.

Thus Angelo became Chaplain-Lieutenant Roncalli.

He served at Turin and later was transferred to his beloved Bergamo which was close to the theater of combat.

On furlough, on weekend pass, he made every effort to do some teaching at the Seminary. When he arrived, on his own time, to teach future priests, he came dressed as any other priest except for the military cap and tunic which covered his cassock.

But what of his experience in the agony of war? What of his thoughts about man's cruelty to man under the mocking camouflage of national flags?

As Pope, he told a group of visiting British officers:

"Your presence first of all evokes in our mind memories which are distant but still remain among the most moving experiences of an already long life.

"The high plateaus of Asiago and those lands washed by the Piave River, endeared to you by graves of so many of your countrymen, were familiar to us during the years when we functioned there as military chaplain. We brought aid to so many of the wounded. To many of the dying we brought comfort and the peace of final absolution. How many fell on the field of honor!"

The long, senseless war "to end all wars", which sapped the valiant spirit of Pope Benedict XV, finally was over.

Lieutenant Roncalli collected four years back pay and quickly became again Father Roncalli of Bergamo Seminary.

He took his mustering-out pay and turned it over to the Rector to be used toward the construction of a new dormitory. It was as simple as that.

He decided, before taking on a full program of teaching, to combine both rest and meditation at a summer villa used by seminarians.

The students heard about his visit and planned a practical joke. Father Roncalli arrived exhausted and ready to retire. He was given a key to what was described as a "cool and comfortable room."

He sought and found the room. He opened the door and found himself in a musty broom closet containing a small bed.

He pondered several moments, sensing the practical joke. But he knew the value of "turning the other cheek."

He got into his pajamas. He knelt down and said his night prayers. He settled into bed and went quietly to sleep.

FROM DIPLOMAT TO PATRIARCH

Pope Benedict XV knew the man for the job.

After World War I, former Chaplain-Lieutenant Roncalli wanted to settle down and become a simple, country school teacher at his beloved seminary in Bergamo.

But Pope Benedict was concerned about the destructive effect of the war on the foreign missions. He wanted some one to help him restore the confidence of distant souls in the sincerity of the Church.

So he plucked Father Angelo right out of Bergamo. He brought him back to Rome and asked him to reorganize the mission groups under the official banner of the Propagation of the Faith.

Pope Benedict had the right idea. He knew that most of the overseas colonies belonging formerly to the losers: Germany, Italy, Japan, would now swell the possessions of the victors: Britain, France, the U.S.A.

In any case, they were undergoing many changes. Freedom was in the air for many African and Asian tribes. They might now be under the protection of the victors, but they would not sit still for long.

Pope Benedict did not want these peoples to suspect or believe that the Church was part of the "deal"—before, during, or after the change of masters.

Benedict wanted the negroes in Africa, the yellow men in Indo-China, the brown men in the South Sea Islands to believe that his missionaries, his priests and nuns sought nothing from them but an audience for teaching the love of Christ.

This was Father Roncalli's assignment: to build confidence in the missions amid a war-torn world.

It was not long after Father Angelo took over his duties that Pope Benedict's poor body was completely worn out.

It is well known that Benedict was a noble sacrifice to the staggering problems of World War I. He was succeeded by the "mountain climber," Achille Ratti, who took the name of Pius XI.

This was the same prelate who had once helped Father Angelo with some library research in Milan. He now encouraged Roncalli to continue the work of reorganizing the missions.

The new Pope emphasized his enthusiasm for continuing this project in two ways:

He named Angelo a Domestic Prelate with the title of Monsignor.

He declared the year 1925 to be a year of Jubilee, a Holy Year during which Rome would provide a wonderful showcase for a new look and a new plan of action in the foreign missions.

Among other things, the duties of the new Monsignor required him to create and act as caretaker for a "wax museum."

This was an exhibit of all the phases of human life involved in the foreign missions. Thus, a modern Francis Xavier in the plain, black robe of a Jesuit would be shown telling the story of Jesus to several colorfully dressed children from India.

Monsignor Roncalli travelled much in the interest of pulling the work of the missions into a highly efficient organization. He moved on official business through Paris, Brussels, Munich, Amsterdam, Vienna.

It was as though his "prep school" training as a major church diplomat was growing in strength and scope.

From those working with him and under him in mission affairs, he asked humbly for advice and suggestions rather than just telling them what to do.

"Speak, speak much," he counseled his colleagues. "I will be very grateful if you would send me detailed reports about everything. But continue, please, to pray for me and for our work."

In March of the Holy Year, Pope Pius was under great pressure from the government of Italy to settle on just how much independence the Vatican would have as a sovereign state.

Pius could handle mild King Victor Emmanuel. But a hot-headed young leader named Mussolini was tipping over Italian "applecarts" in the background.

In the great Balkan city of Sofia, Bulgaria, the Pope's Apostolic Delegate had died. The rights and peace of 50,000 Roman Catholics were in danger because of explosive internal problems.

Pius needed an international trouble-shooter in Bulgaria.

He needed some one who could protect the Church and the faithful in the Balkans while the Pope concentrated on straightening out his problems with the Italian government.

Without hesitation Pius called on Monsignor Roncalli to take on this difficult assignment.

He appointed him Vicar Apostolic for the Latin Rite Catholics of Bulgaria. This appointment also made him titular Bishop of Areopolis with the title of Archbishop.

"Archbishop" Roncalli was consecrated in Rome by Cardinal Tacci and left for Sofia almost immediately.

The new Archbishop could not have been given a tougher assignment.

Bombs of political assassination were bursting in Sofia when he arrived. One of these killed the Prime Minister.

Roman Catholics were in the minority and were held somewhat in suspicion and contempt by Orthodox

Catholics who were the officially recognized group of the stormy Bulgarian kingdom.

Archbishop Roncalli noticed one thing in Bulgaria right away. Roman Catholics, originally instructed by French clergy and nuns, were reciting their Rosary and other prayers in French.

This was something which set them apart from their fellow citizens who prayed in their native tongue.

The new "Apostolic Visitor" changed this custom immediately. Prayers of Roman Catholics were henceforth said in Bulgarian.

Love and care were what Bulgarian Catholics needed to cement them together with their fellow citizens and their nation.

This Archbishop Roncalli knew because of what Pius XI had said to a group of Bulgarian travelers: "He will have my ears that I should hear you, my lips that I should talk to you and my heart that you should feel how much I love you."

Roncalli sought the bond of love with the clergy and faithful of the Orthodox Church also. In his heart was deep belief in eventual religious unity, but in his actions were friendship and unselfish service.

He walked amid earthquakes to bring help to his new "parishioners." He visited long-bearded monks in hospitals and lavished them with such kindness that one said: "Our own authorities would not have cared for us with as much love as you."

He visited parishes in remote mountain places where ruthless bandit chieftains passed the word to let him alone. He dwelt with the wounded war veterans in their sick wards. Always he worked for unity and friendship through good example.

King Boris knew and admired him, as did the Queen and the Prime Minister. Soon they visited Pope Pius and told him about his remarkable messenger in Sofia.

Who knew better than the Pope the kind of man he had in Sofia?

Ten years passed.

That job was done, the job of good relations between the Vatican and Bulgaria, the job of solid approaches to religious unity, the job of friendship and understanding between Latin and Orthodox Catholics.

Now the Pope sent Archbishop Roncalli to do the same work in Turkey and Greece as Apostolic Delegate to those countries.

Before Roncalli left Sofia, he spoke in the jam-packed Cathedral of St. Josif. It was Christmas Day. He spoke of peace: peace in the heart, peace in the family, the nation, the world.

"Bulgarian Catholics could always reconcile their faith with their love for their country and respect for its institutions."

This is what he had worked for and what he had helped achieve for the people and the nation.

In Turkey and Greece his career was similar.

He got the Turkish Catholics to pray in their native tongue. He made friends with the strong, ruthless premier, Kemal Ataturk. Roncalli eventually convinced Ataturk that Turkish Christians loved their country just as much as Mohammedans and others.

Ataturk soon thought enough of Roncalli to honor his suggestion concerning the great basilica of Santa Sophia. This beautiful, historically famous church in Istanbul was built by Emperor Justinian in the ninth century. Istanbul was then known as Constantinople, the center of political power in the Holy Roman Empire.

After the Mohammedans conquered Turkey, the holy basilica became a mosque. And in modern times the Turks, who had overthrown the Moslems, planned to turn the basilica into a museum.

Archbishop Roncalli worked to convince Ataturk that the basilica should be kept as a historical monument rather than a museum. As a monument its beauty would be kept intact and could be visited in much of its original holy atmosphere and splendor.

The Apostolic Delegate went to great pains to show the government that many paintings and much art work now concealed under Moslem embellishments were priceless in the heritage of beauty that belongs to all mankind.

Ataturk finally saw the merit in Roncalli's argument. The basilica was declared a historical monument and thus retained much of the atmosphere of a shrine.

In 1939, Angelo's great sponsor, Pope Pius XI, died.

The Apostolic Delegate preached of Pius' great desire at a memorial service in Istanbul's Holy Ghost Basilica.

"The unity of all Christians was the most secret longing of Pope Pius XI," Roncalli told the distinguished congregation.

This, too, was Angelo's most secret longing, he was later to reveal as Pope John XXIII.

The Second World War: Hitler invades Poland! The Japanese bomb Pearl Harbor!

The Apostolic Delegate remained in Turkey at the will and pleasure of the new Pope: ascetic, scholarly Pius XII.

With the onrush of the great war, Angelo found himself in a Hollywood setting of spies and international intrigue. With his amazing flexibility, Roncalli seemed as much at home in such an atmosphere as the cinema's Humphrey Bogart.

The Archbishop's "intrigues," if they can be called that, were for Christ. In constant contact with the Vatican, he was able to use his diplomatic skill to help countless Jewish refugees escape the Nazis and seek safe haven in Palestine.

German, British and other foreign agents trailed him about the Turkish Capitol. "I never could find out whether they followed and watched me or one another," Roncalli commented.

Although there was no question of the Vatican's preference for the allied cause, Archbishop Roncalli stayed in touch with the German Ambassador, Franz Von Papen, with one objective in view: the welfare of the Church and the people in Nazi Germany.

Von Papen pleaded that the Vatican must recognize the difference between the inhuman Hitler regime and the German people themselves.

Roncalli saw the merit in this plea, from the Christian point of view. He made this view clear to Pope Pius XII.

Athens and Greece were the Delegate's next field of labor.

He visited and consoled the wounded and prisoners of war of all nations.

He was deeply moved by his experience at an Italian prisoner of war camp, recalling his own service in the Italian army in World War I.

An Italian Corporal rushed out to meet him as he entered the camp. Officers sought to restrain him but Roncalli moved toward the soldier.

"What can I do for you, Corporal?" Roncalli asked.

The soldier went down on one knee, kissed the Archbishop's ring and said: "Your Excellency, I do this for all of us."

Roncalli became a well-known figure around the Greek Orthodox monasteries and heeded their pleas to intercede with the Turkish government for their oppressed brother monks in Turkey.

"The stones spoke, . . ." Angelo tells us, in his efforts to prepare the ground for unity. He simply acted as though unity was as natural as rain. This sweet, humble attitude, combined with constant service and understanding of Orthodox Greeks and Monks earned rich dividends.

Distrust, suspicion of the Orthodox steadily declined.

Such was this "melting of the ice" that in 1945 the Catholic Archbishop of Athens and the Orthodox Archbishop commemorated the end of the war together on the same platform.

Late in 1944, the summons came from Pius XII for Roncalli to help heal the gaping wounds of France.

He was appointed Papal Nuncio to France where the war-time government under General De Gaulle was rather cool toward the Vatican.

This strain existed because the Church, in the interest of protecting the faithful even in enemy countries, had maintained an attitude of mild neutrality between two bitter French factions led by General Petain and General De Gaulle respectively.

Such neutrality gave the French Communists and professional Catholic-haters the opportunity to attack Roncalli. They were really attacking the Church and did not need much encouragement to do so.

The Nuncio saw in the Archbishop of Toulouse, Monsignor Saliege, a fine chance to show the good will of the Church toward those who fought the Nazis.

Saliege was a Bishop of uncommon bravery. His was a true image of the religious nature of France and the French. He had for years publicly denounced Hitler and the Nazi butchers. He had a tremendous spiritual following among the French and continually called on them to do penance and be true to their great Catholic religious traditions.

Even though his body was almost totally paralyzed, Saliege insisted on being carried into the Cathedral to preach against the Nazis and the French traitors who had supported them.

"Who Shall Bear The Flame?" Saliege asked in the title of his book, published here in America after the war. One answer is, of course, that he himself bore that flame before all the world—the flame of freedom and justice under God.

Archbishop Roncalli, on his arrival in France, soon saw this man as the symbol of a reborn Catholic France. He asked Pope Pius XII to make Saliege a Cardinal. It was done.

Roncalli personally brought the red hat to Saliege in Toulouse.

The Nuncio remained in France nine years, healing and binding the wounds of the nation with full cooperation from the Pope.

Post-war President Vincent Auriol, a non-Catholic, tells us sometimes he would meet his friend Archbishop Roncalli in a hotel lobby. "After a few moments, people would be down on their knees all around him," Auriol revealed.

To save post-war France from Communism and indifference toward Catholicism, many priests put on civilian clothes and mingled among the people as fellow workers.

They were known as "Worker Priests."

The intention of the movement was fine and the results good. But many worker priests could not avoid getting involved in politics much to the detriment of their religious duties.

The Vatican was worried. Archbishop Roncalli saw the merit of the movement and tried to adjust the program. But when the worker priests got involved in Communist-controlled labor unions, the Pope had to dissolve the movement.

Yet even opponents of the church were impressed with Roncalli's patience and charity toward the worker priests.

Said Edouard Herriot, a former Premier of France and a known anti-clerical: "If all the priests were like Roncalli, we would have no trouble with the Church."

That was the idea! And Pius XII understood it! So had in varying degrees, Pius X, Benedict XV, and Pius XI, before him.

The United Nations was forming its ranks big and strong, immediately after World War II. Its UNESCO section, dealing with the problems of education, social welfare, and culture among the nations, needed a representative from the Vatican.

Who but Archbishop Roncalli was named to the post!

Roncalli advised UNESCO, with all its noble enthusiasms, to proceed slowly and not try to accomplish everything at once.

"The creation of the world was accomplished in six days, the book of Genesis tells us. For each day there was a precisely defined task.

"Beyond all the victories and triumphs of human science," Archbishop Roncalli told UNESCO Catholics in 1952, "shines the gospel of Christ which contains the elements of civilization. This is the faith of the Christian and the Catholic who works for an international organization like UNESCO."

The man who carried the Red Hat to Cardinal Saliege was now to receive it himself.

In late November, 1952, word came through that Pope Pius XII had elevated Angelo Roncalli to the College of Cardinals.

The village of Sotto il Monte, a little township in the province of Bergamo, Italy, birthplace of Pope John XXIII. Atop the hill to the right of the photo is the church of St. John, a favorite retreat of the young Father Angelo Roncalli.

Views of the Roncalli home in Sotto il Monte where John XXIII was born.

Alfred and Joseph, two of the Pope's brothers.

Alfred Roncalli busy with his farm duties.

Zaverio Roncalli, a third brother.

John XXIII's father, John Baptist Roncalli, was a sharecropper
on the lands of a local nobleman.

His mother, Marianna Roncalli

The ancient stone and brick facade of the Church of the
Holy Spirit, Pope John's boyhood Church.

In the early days of the Second
Vatican Council, Pope John told me
that the restoration of the old
parish Church would be the
"best personal gift that
I could receive."

Photo of the seminarian Angelo Roncalli (center)
taken in 1901 when he was twenty years old.

Sergeant Roncalli, officer in the
Italian Medical Corps in 1915.

In World War I the future Pope was promoted to the
rank of Sergeant-major and finally to chaplaincy
with the rank of lieutenant.
Reflecting on his years of active military service,
John XXIII recalled, "How great was the grace of experience
I received in dedication, sacrifice and in the understanding
of life and the priestly apostolate."

From 1925 to 1945 the Vatican assigned Archbishop Roncalli
to difficult and delicate diplomatic positions in the East.
In January, 1945 Pope Pius XII appointed him
Papal Nuncio to France and in the consistory of January, 1953
elevated him to the rank of Cardinal.

According to an ancient privilege accorded to the heads of the French government, the red biretta was bestowed on Nuncio Roncalli by the President of the French Republic, Vincent Auriol at the Elysee Palace.

Pope Pius XII and the future John XXIII

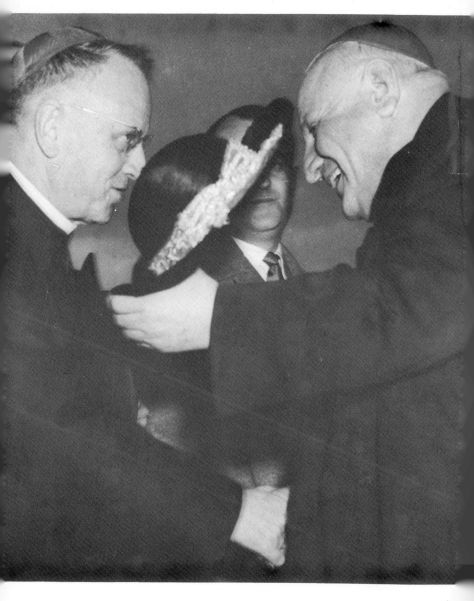

The arrival of the Patriarch of Venice at Lourdes in 1958
to celebrate the centenary of the apparitions of Our Lady
to St. Bernadette and to consecrate the underground basilica
dedicated to St. Pius X.

On October 9, 1958, the world was saddened by the death of Pope Pius XII. Shortly afterwards Cardinal Roncalli left Venice for Rome and the conclave that would elect the new Pope. The Venetian faithful multiplied their farewells to their beloved Patriarch who was deeply moved. "Everyone wishes me well. For me the best wish is that I may be able to return to Venice in two weeks." Here, Cardinal Roncalli is shown entering the Conclave.

At the end of the third day of the conclave, October 28, 1958,
wisps of white smoke rose upward from the chimney
of the Sistine Chapel. Later, in a voice broken
with emotion, Cardinal Canali announced to the world
the anxiously awaited news: "I announce to you a great joy:
we have a Pope: the most eminent and reverend
Lord Cardinal Roncalli, who has chosen the name of John XXIII.

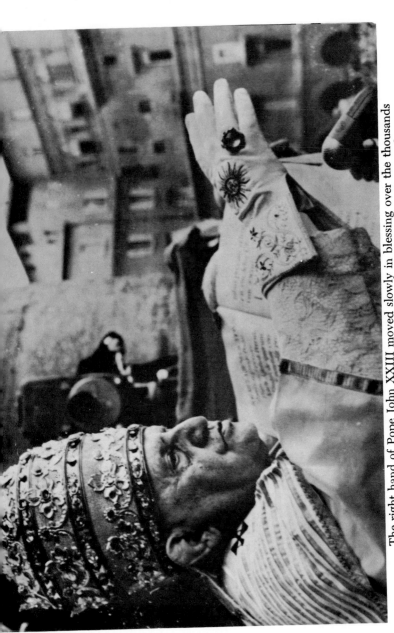

The right hand of Pope John XXIII moved slowly in blessing over the thousands gathered in St. Peter's Square, as the newly crowned Pontiff gave the traditional blessing "Urbi et Orbi" – "To the City and the World" – after his coronation on November 4, 1958.

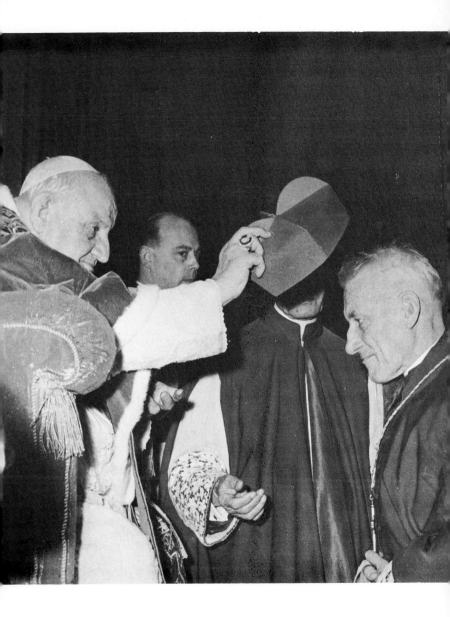

At his first consistory, December, 1958,
Pope John imposed the red biretta
on myself and twenty-two other Cardinals.

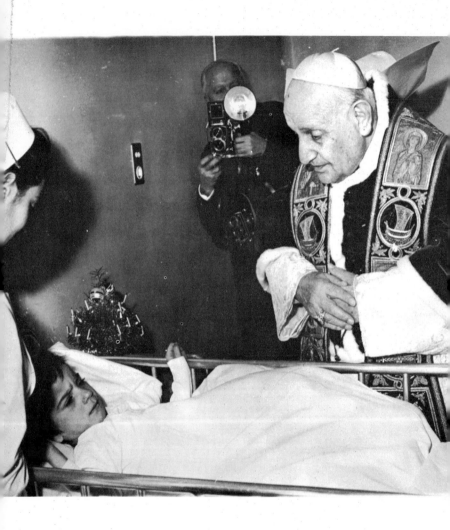

Christmas Day, 1958, Pope John visited the infants and children at
Gesù Bambino Hospital in Rome.

Pope John at prayer in the Basilica of St. Paul.
During this visit to the Basilica on the feast of the
Conversion of St. Paul in 1959, he publicly announced the
proposed Ecumenical Council for the restoration
of Christian Unity.

Pope John XXIII visiting the North American College accompanied by the Rector, Archbishop Martin O'Connor (right) and the former Vice Rector, Msgr. George Schlicte, on the occasion of the Seminary's 100th Anniversary.

His Holiness visiting the College museum. In the background
are photographs of the visit of Pope Pius XII when
he blessed and dedicated the new seminary building.

Students of the North American College presented the
Holy Father with a Chalice and vestments as a token of
their love and appreciation for his visit.
Pope John surprised everyone when he answered the Rector's
address in English. He then bestowed his blessing
on the entire gathering.

The news had a mixed effect on Angelo. Joy, yes, but sadness also. It meant he would have to leave France where he had grown to love the country, the people, his work.

A future, great Pope was now to express his basic humility in the belief that he would be buried in a Vatican office for the rest of his career.

"Now I have to leave Paris. I have to leave France and all this is painful for me. It is painful to think that I should end my life among Roman paperwork in the Offices and Congregations."

Elevated to the Cardinalate about the same time as Roncalli was the elderly Archbishop and Patriarch, Carlo Agostini of Venice.

It was not long before a great gondola, draped in majestic black, was moving slowly through the Grand Canal of Venice.

As monks chanted the Office of the Dead, and the great brass tongues of the Cathedral of St. Mark tolled, the funeral fleet moved through the exotic, ancient city of mercantile splendor.

Lying in state on the "Gondola of the Dead" was Patriarch and Cardinal-Elect, Carlo Agostini.

Who would succeed him amid the magnificently structured an exquisitely carved stones of Venice? Who would be the next Patriarch of Venice?

"Boomlay! Bong-a-long!" lamented the great brass tongues of St. Mark's Cathedral. All across the gorgeous Italian city of canals and palaces, scores of church bells took up the gloomy refrain.

"*WHO WILL SUCCEED HIM? WHO? WHO? WHO?*" asked the bells.

"THAT ALL MAY BE ONE!"

To be Patriarch and Archbishop of Venice would be enough power and glory for almost any man.

Surely this seemed more than enough for Angelo Roncalli.

He had expected at age seventy-one to finish out his priestly career as a sort of high class office clerk in some Vatican bureau.

Now, in the year 1953, most of the splendor of ancient and modern Venice was his to command.

But he was never fond of giving commands.

He was still the same Roncalli who took the soldier off company punishment and sent him out to frolic in the sunshine with his "buddies." He was the same Roncalli the world had known in Bulgaria, in Turkey, Greece, in France. He was a man of action, a man of total Christian love, a man of humble, good example.

Right away he told the Venetians what kind of Bishop they could expect him to be: "In beholding your Patriarch, seek the priest, the minister of grace and nothing else, because he wishes to express in his ministry this vocation given to him by God."

He walked the streets of the city like any pedestrian, except that he was clad in simple clerical garb: a black cassock, topcoat and the flat hat with small dome, so typical of Roman priestly attire.

Only occasionally did he ride in a gondola. He did not choose to own one himself. When he rode the "watery streets", he borrowed a ride in a police launch or paid his fare on a "floating streetcar."

He improved and renovated the great basilica of St. Mark. He uncovered that Saint's tomb so the people could see it while they were worshipping at Mass or visiting in prayer.

He personally visited every parish in his Archdiocese. He began construction of a new seminary.

He was ever the modest country priest when it came to his relations with the Bishops who ran the dioceses under his archdiocesan leadership.

Once when he accepted an invitation to dinner in the home of a friend who lived in an outlying diocese he showed his ever-present humility. He phoned the Bishop of the diocese and asked his permission to go into that area for dinner.

His private secretary was the same young, keen-minded, profoundly loyal priest who was later to stand beside him at the throne of St. Peter.

In the office of the Patriarch this priest, Monsignor Loris Capovilla, knew that there were no rigid appointment schedules for Angelo Roncalli.

Capovilla was told to let any one enter who wanted to do so. The Patriarch's reason for this is clear in his own words:

"Someone may want to go to Confession to me."

Pope Pius XII still called on him to lend the papal dignity to international events.

In October of 1954, Cardinal Roncalli served as Papal Legate to the Marian Year Congress in Beirut, Lebanon. In March of 1958, he was sent to Lourdes to officiate at the 100th Anniversary of the appearances of Our Lady to St. Bernadette.

On both occasions there were happy reunions with diplomats and government leaders he had known in Bulgaria, Turkey, Greece and France.

We can be sure it was not hard for him to be a "regular guy" on these occasions since he was a "regular fellow" most of the time anyway. We can guess that he wanted to put people at their ease by being informal with them; we can also surmise that he wanted these diplomats and public officials to feel at home in telling him what was really going on in their affairs of state.

The Communists in Venice tried to take advantage of his good nature by spreading the word that he had united with them to stop the spread of unemployment.

While he was all for stopping unemployment, he let it be known in a public statement that "negotiations between Catholics and Marxists have never been nor could ever be, opened in Venice."

However, he continued to be respectful of those who honestly had a difference of opinion with the Church. He publicly welcomed the members of the Socialist Party who came to Venice for their national congress in 1957 and let them know that he, like all Venetians, "knew the value of hospitality."

Once at a children's summer camp he was entertained by a skit which made fun of the somewhat odd actions of elderly folks.

In his mid-seventies himself, he found himself laughing heartily at the mimicry and antics of the young. He still managed to strike a sober note with the children, however, commenting:

"You are saying the same things about old folks that we used to say when we were children. That is all right. Some day children will be saying the same things about you."

The increasing illness of the saintly, ascetic Pope Pius XII ended in his death on October 9, 1958. He who had walked so bravely amid the German bombardment of Rome to comfort his people, now went bravely amid the bombs of mortality to his heavenly reward.

Cardinal Roncalli left for Rome by train to attend the funeral and help elect a new Pope. He promised to return to Venice in fifteen days.

Roncalli's friend, the late Pius X, had also intended to return to Venice. He had been Patriarch of Venice and left for Rome by train on the death of Leo XIII.

Many of Angelo's parishioners and friends hoped and believed that something important would prevent his return to St. Mark's.

There was something in the air, in the wind whipping among the Cathedral bells, in the carefree songs of the gondoliers.

"The Cardinal will not return," all of Venice seemed to say with a little sadness and yet a lyrical joy of anticipation.

He had promised to return in fifteen days. On the nineteenth day of his absence he was elected Pope by the 78th Conclave of the College of Cardinals.

At the moment of acceptance of his election, as the white smoke puffed and billowed above the Sistine Chapel, his words were humble but strong.

"I tremble and am afraid. My poorness and littleness fills me with confusion. But I see in the votes of my eminent brother Cardinals the sign of the will of God. Therefore I accept the election. I bow my head and bend my back to the Cross."

Cardinal Tisserant, Dean of the College of Cardinals, then asked: "By what name shall you be called?"

"I shall be called John. This name is dear to us because it is the name of our father. It is dear to us because it is the name of the humble parish church where we were baptized. . . ."

Great was the joy in the world, and among the thousands he blessed publicly in St. Peter's Square.

"HABEMUS PAPAM!" "We have a Pope!" announced Cardinal Canali on the balcony overlooking St.

Peter's square. The word went around the world with the sweep and power of modern electronics.

Congratulations poured in from the great and the small: President Eisenhower, Queen Elizabeth, the Chief Rabbi of Israel, the Archbishop of Canterbury, the Patriarch of the Russian Orthodox Church.

But the new Pope John was still the same Angelo Roncalli. He did not linger overlong on the balcony for the plaudits of the crowd. He was, as always, the man of action. He retired to the papal apartment and went right to work.

Many official messages went out. But one special message went to his relatives and loved ones at a village called Sotte Il Monte, Under the Mountain. He would see them all in person at his Coronation.

The holy splendor of the Papal Coronation took place on November 4th.

Now the man of action moved.

Within a month of his election he created twenty-five new Cardinals, raising the membership to seventy-five. This broke a tradition that was four hundred years old.

One of the first to be named was the Archbishop of Milan, Giovanni Battista Montini. Montini had been a close aide of Pius XII before becoming Archbishop and had been prominently mentioned as a Papal possibility. He was famed far and wide as a friend of the working-man who espoused strong liberal thinking in the social order and in the Church itself.

Physically he resembled Pius XII, lean and burning with fervor for the good of man and the glory of God. But in a deeper way he resembled the plump and jolly Pope John. That was in his sense of the times, of the need for change in the Church in order to compete with the swift and efficient paganism of the world.

In the mind and as a man of action, to sum it up, Montini was very close to Pope John. The Penguin and the Arctic Tern, you might say, but each alert to the best interests of the Church in a ruthless, carnal world.

"This Montini could have been Pope," it was said. Pope John generously kept alive that possibility by promptly making him a Cardinal.

Two American Archbishops were among those receiving the Red Hat at that time—myself and the late Archbishop O'Hara of Philadelphia.

Pope John quickly proved that he would be no "Buddha". He refused to languish on the papal throne and wait for people to come to him. He did not wish to be a "caretaker" of the church and its old traditions.

He went to his "parishioners" as he saw them in his "parish of the world."

As in Venice, he soon walked the streets of the Vatican and the City of Rome itself. He went to the Vatican radio station unannounced. He bounced into visits at the various colleges and seminaries under his wing. He roamed through hospitals, consoling and blessing, with particular attention to sick little children.

"Tears, sorrow and the sufferings of men must not be wasted, because they have a purpose," he told the sick and the infirm.

He stunned and then moved the world with his visit on the day after Christmas to Rome's city jail, known as Regina Caeli.

This was the first visit of a Pope to a jail since 1870.

Such was the surprise of the Pope's visit that the jail superintendent shouted "WHO?" when he heard that the Pontiff was coming.

The warden later calmed down and commented that Bishops didn't need any special pass to enter a prison, and that "the Bishop of Rome, of course, can come any time."

And he did. He walked right into that prison, announcing to the four tiers of cell blocks, to murderers, thieves and wastrels of all sorts: "Well, I have come. You have seen me. I have fixed my eyes upon yours. I have joined my heart to your heart."

The Pope actually joined "heart to heart" by telling the prisoners a story of how his uncle was once put in jail for "poaching."

In his tour of good cheer, he came to a section of the prison where special bars confined murderers and robbers who were considered hopeless and dangerous.

"Open up the gates!" Pope John said. "Do not bar me from them. They are all children of the Lord."

When he gave his final blessing to the prisoners, an on-the-spot reporter tells us the whole place was in tears. The prisoners were weeping, as were the jailers, and the warden; Good Pope John, too, was crying. Because of him great joy sundered the iron gray misery of the prison and all seemed richly possessed by the gift of tears.

A wonderful postscript to this incident occurred on the Feast of the Epiphany. With his compliments, Pope John sent the entire prison population, convicts and guards alike, a complete chicken dinner. Tin plates and cups were put aside and the sumptuous meal was served on white paper plates with wine in white paper cups.

The prison chaplain later observed that the Pope's signal attention to the prison had a definite effect: "In the overwhelming majority of cases it made a positive impression. The Pope did not pass in vain."

Pope John was a man of a thousand jests and a thousand human acts. Once he was asked: "How many people are working in Vatican City?"

"About half," the Pope answered, without hesitation.

The humane side of his thinking showed itself when the Pope granted special financial preference to all lay Vatican employees with five children or more.

Speaking amid a group of Roman street cleaners, the Pope said: "You must be happy, free as you are from the worry of handling large sums of money. It is the rich who have those worries."

He told a group of farmers that he would have been a tiller of the soil had he not become a priest: "If the Lord had not called me, I would have been one of you. I would be here with you asking the Holy Father for his blessing."

He said to an American photographer who had just snapped his photo: "Would you send me the picture? No one ever sends me any pictures."

In a chat with a Rome policeman, formerly of Naples, he spoke of his great liking for Neapolitans and related this anecdote: "Visiting Naples as a young priest, I took a taxi to visit a certain section of the city. The driver addressed me with the title of Excellency and although I had promised him a good tip, he insisted on taking me a roundabout way so that he could build up the meter fare."

Recalling his army service, he once said to a captain of the Swiss Guard: "I should defer to you. I was only a sergeant."

To an American nurse he expressed his interest in the design of her white cap, which he jokingly described as a "miter."

In a more serious vein he asked about her family in the U.S.A. When she said she was one of fifteen children, he replied: "Where there are many children, the food must be plentiful. The Lord always blessed a full pot. He certainly blessed your family and I do, too."

On one occasion he asked me: "Are you a theologian?" Knowing he would get the point I replied, "Your Holiness, the only theology I remember is in Catechism No. 2. All my priesthood has been spent in helping others." "Shake hands," he said, "you will never have any problems."

On another occasion, pointing to the then Msgr. Tom Ryan, now a bishop, who was serving as interpreter, His Holiness said to me, "He is my teacher. I am the best pupil in his English class." Smiling all over, he added, "Know why?" Then came the answer: "I am the only one he has."

Schooled by this Irish Monsignor, the Pope labored hard at gaining a facility in the speaking of English. He devoutly desired to speak to Americans in their native tongue.

He eventually spoke in English at the hundredth anniversary of the North American College in Rome and created quite a stir. I was present in my capacity as a Trustee of the College.

The next day, before eight hundred American Churchmen, he apologized for his bad English. He spoke, this time, in Italian.

He had the right sense of the difficulties of learning the English language.

"We are annoyed with English—not with the language itself, but with the rules for vowels. In fact, if one studies English, he finds that some vowels are pronounced one way and then pronounced another way. But it happens that often there are exceptions. And, as a result, one vowel that one believes is pronounced in one way is pronounced in another—only because it is followed by a certain vowel or preceded by a certain vowel.

"So," he concluded, provoking laughter with a shrug of his shoulders, "We are speaking Italian today."

I was in that audience. I realized the Pope's efforts to learn English were an indication of his love for the United States and all English—speaking peoples.

"That all may be one!"

The unity of all Christian religions—this was the deepest desire of the Pope's life. He had sensed it under the reigns of Pius XI and Pius XII, who like him, wanted this unity so intensely.

Now as Pope he would make an affirmative move to do something about it.

It has been said that the Roman Curia, ever conservative, was not enthusiastic about Pope John's intention to call a Vatican Council in the interest of religious unity and for updating the pastoral life of the Church.

One Curia official reportedly said to the Pope: "We can't possibly get a council ready by 1963."

"All right," Pope John said. "We'll have it in 1962."

He was as good as his word.

During his observance of the Conversion of St. Paul, January 25, 1959, he let his intentions be publicly known. He announced to the world that he had decided to call the first Ecumenical Council in nearly a century.

This would take place on October 11, 1962, and there was much work of organization and preparation to accomplish before that date.

The Pope moved in a spirit of "make haste slowly."

The Council would bring together close to 2500 Cardinals, Archbishops, Abbots and other Council Fathers. It would be the most representative worldwide gathering of Church leaders in history.

The Pope expected much of the Council but expressed only reasonable hopes for its achievements. His main hope, he said, was that: "The Church, Spouse of Christ, may strengthen still more her divine energies and extend her beneficial influence in still greater measure to the minds of men."

His hopes and dreams for the Council were a logical extension of the family love he had expressed practically as reorganizer of the foreign missions, Apostolic Delegate to Bulgaria, Turkey, and Greece, and as Nuncio to France. In striving to bring alienated religious groups to harmony with Rome he had fulfilled not only his own wishes but those of the then reigning Popes. As Pope himself he wanted to take a great stride forward to the distant but hoped-for goal of one fold, one shepherd.

He issued encyclicals; he beatified and canonized saints.

His first official letter to the world-wide faithful was "Ad Petri Cathedram", which invited separated brethren to return to the Catholic Church. The encyclical also appealed for renewed efforts for peace in the world.

At the centenary celebration of the North American Seminary in Rome, he made, in English, the announcement of the coming beatification of Mother Elizabeth Seton, American foundress of the Sisters of Charity.

"Il Papa Simpatico," the warm-hearted Pope, as he was now so well-known, gave cordial audiences to the great of the world, including: President Charles De Gaulle of France, Chancellor Konrad Adenauer of Germany, President Manuel Prado of Peru, President Arturo Frondizi of Argentina, the King and Queen of Siam, Queen Elizabeth of England, King Baudouin and Queen Fabiola of Belgium, President Constantine Karamalis of Greece, Premier Amintore Fanfani of Italy, U.S. Vice President Lyndon Johnson, and many others.

He also gave a cordial audience to former President Eisenhower at which he and Ike had a hearty laugh together.

The Pope hesitated to read the formal speech which had been prepared for him, out of deference to his most distinguished guest. He glanced at the text, turned to Ike, smiling, and said in Italian: "This is gonna be a beaut!"

When his remark was translated, Ike threw back his head and roared with laughter. The Pope joined in the mirth and the photographers snapped their pictures for the whole world to see.

On March 28, 1960, John XXIII created seven more new Cardinals; on January 16, 1961, he added four more; and, finally, on March 19, 1962, he elevated ten more Bishops to the rank of Prince of the Church. This brought the total enrollment of the "College" to a historic total of eighty-seven members.

Among those given the Red Hat by the Pope of One World and One Church were the first Cardinals to be named for Japan and the Philippines: namely Peter Cardinal Tatsuo-Doi, Archbishop of Tokyo and Rufino Cardinal Santos, Archbishop of Manila.

Deeply aware of the brave new world out there, the Pope also included a Red Hat for the first negro Cardinal of all time. He is Laurian Cardinal Rugambwa, Bishop of Bukoba, Tanganyika.

One of John's most distinguished and thoughtful encyclicals, issued on July 14, 1961, is "Mater et Magistra," translated "Mother and Teacher."

In it he gave recognition to the arrival of social welfare as a permanent item in the program of various governments. For example, here in the U.S.A., Social Security pensions, once looked on as a socialistic program, are now highly respectable. He talked about "regulated" socialization.

He was also unhappy about the "flight from the farm" in a highly mechanized society. As a son of farmers, he knew the importance of agriculture in feeding the world and stabilizing family life. He pleaded for a reemphasis of the beauty and the dignity of farm life. He called also for more help on the part of the "rich nations" toward the "poor nations."

The time for the Ecumenical Council was at hand.

Reforms in Church Law were important in order to pave the way to religious unity.

The Pope reminded those who would attend the Council that the present Code of Canon Law has been in force for more than forty years and is now outdated on many questions. "It must therefore be brought up to date to meet the needs and circumstances of present day life," Pope John insisted.

"The Church is living," he advised the Council. "She is not just the custodian of a museum. Though the Church has great respect for what is ancient, beautiful and good, her first concern is souls. That is why the Church intends to give dioceses a better ecclesiastical and juridical structure."

On October 11, 1962, the Ecumenical Council opened with thirty-five non-Catholic observers and guests present. These men, mostly clergy, represented seventeen Protestant and Orthodox groups.

Pope John said to them in a special audience: "There burns in my heart the intention of working and suffering to hasten the hour when for all men the prayer of Jesus at the Last Supper will have reached its fulfillment: Ut Unum Sint—that all may be one."

The Council itself in one of its first acts declared: "All men are brothers irrespective of the race or nation to which they belong."

The work of the Council proceeded throughout the first session with some last-ditch objections to reform and renewal. But the time had come for changes in the Church's approach to the world, in her pastoral life, not in her unchangeable doctrines. There was no possibility of holding back the trends.

In April of 1963, Pope John issued his momentous encyclical, "Pacem in Terris," Peace on Earth, which captured the imagination and sympathy of the civilized world.

Published purposely on Holy Thursday, the letter to mankind emphasized the words of Christ at the Last Supper: "Love one another."

The encyclical called for the settlement of controversy through meetings and negotiations. The Pope exhorted the nations to overcome racial and national barriers. He called for general disarmament among the world powers—all with an eye to human freedom and human dignity.

Praising this encyclical at the centennial celebration at Boston College, the late beloved President John F. Kennedy, whose assassination brought the whole world to its knees, said—after commenting on it, "This encyclical of Pope John makes me proud to be a Catholic." Before John died, he bequeathed to the late President an autographed copy of that encyclical with some other personal tokens of esteem. His Holiness had hoped to present these mementos to the President of the United States when he visited Rome. But when that visit took place Pope John had been called to his reward. I had the privilege of presenting to my dear friend these gifts when President Kennedy came to the Eternal City shortly after the election of Pope Paul VI. The two "Johns"—John the Pope and John the assassinated leader of the free world— are now by the grace of God in the mansions of Heaven.

Earlier in March, Pope John had received Khrushchev's daughter and son-in-law in cordial audience. Alexei Adzhubei, the Premier's son-in-law, and distinguished editor of "Pravda", told the world press he had been greatly impressed by the Pope.

This visit seemed to be a practical demonstration of what could be normally done to relieve world tensions. It came as a modest but strong preface to the issuance of the Pope's encyclical on peace.

In a flood of messages from the great and powerful of the world, John's encyclical on peace was hailed as an historical document which surely must help the nations avert their collision course toward mutual nuclear destruction.

The Pope had been ill in November of 1962.

At Christmas time he had talked cheerfully of his hopes that the Ecumenical Council might be finished by Christmas of 1963. "One year is a long time," he said. "I may not be here. But if I'm not, there certainly will be another Pope."

Shortly after this sad "immortal longing" was expressed, Pope John was named "Man of the Year: 1962" by "Time" Magazine. He was the only man of religion ever to be so named.

By spring, his great vitality waned and it was easily apparent to all that he was seriously ill. His illness was soon revealed as a stomach tumor, and repeated blood transfusions gradually became inadequate.

A few days before his death, he said to his doctors: "Don't worry about me. My bags are packed and I'm ready to go."

He died, on June 3, 1963, voicing the hope that prayers being offered in his behalf could include a special intention. He expressed the hope that his death would win blessings for the Church, for the Ecumenical Council and for peace.

So, he finally went, good Pope John, jolly Pope John, wise Pope John, saintly Pope John!

What a Pope! What a man! What a priest! What a saint!

All of us—white, black, yellow, and brown; all the Catholics, all the Protestants, all the Jews, all creeds, all colors, all unbelievers, all states in life—we are all so much better off because we were here when Pope John was here!

In his lifetime as Bishop, Archbishop, Patriarch and Pope he had two pectoral crosses. He left one to me. He also honored me by mentioning me in his diary.

The cross I gave to a community of poor nuns who have suffered much under a hostile government.

The diary reference to me I have not seen. It is sufficient for me that I knew this great man of God whom everyone loved.

I pray that one day his name will adorn the calendars and the altars of the Church to which he was a great consolation.

MASTER BRIDGE BUILDER

Shortly after Angelo Giuseppe Roncalli was ordained a priest he had a private audience with Pope Pius X. Having given the young Levite his blessing, the saintly Pontiff counselled Father Roncalli "to live so that his priesthood would prove a consolation to the Church." Accepting the challenge of a future saint, he became not only a consolation to the Church but to the entire world.

Above and beyond his various ecclesiastical, diplomatic and episcopal positions prior to his election as Sovereign Pontiff, Pope John XXIII was at all times and in every sense of the word an exemplary priest, a good shepherd united by love and service to those within and without the fold of the Catholic Church. "I must think," he once said, "that whoever calls on me might also be coming to confess his sins."

These are the most priestly words that any priest could utter. They are a tribute to Angelo Roncalli, the priest, the mediator between God and man, who in our time became a Spiritual Father to all mankind.

In the fall of 1958 as he approached his seventy-seventh birthday, and while Patriarch of Venice, an office once held by St. Pius X, he was elected Pope and took the name of John XXIII. John was his father's name. John the Baptist was one of his favorite saints. John was the most popular name taken by popes prior to the fifteenth century. St. John Lateran Basilica is the mother church of the Diocese of Rome and there out of respect for his own desire he willed to be entombed. Selecting the name, John XXIII, he observed that former pontiffs of the same name reigned for only a short time. A similar experience awaited him. Advanced in years, young in spirit, he governed the Church less than five years. But within that time he became one of the most beloved, unique, and in a constructive way, revolutionary Pontiff in history.

The word "Pontiff" comes from the Latin word "Pontifex" meaning a bridge builder. In the spiritual order of this atomic and chaotic age a master bridge builder was urgently needed. During the long course of nineteen centuries the Gospel of Christ has been accepted by only one-third of the human race. Great sacrifice and labor, sweat and tears were behind this accomplishment. But today entire regions, like Asia Minor and the countries of North Africa, which were once Christian are inhabited by populations which are for the most part non-Christian. Elsewhere millions of the followers of Christ are undergoing a persistent and an eroding persecution under a militant atheism which endangers the faith and the Christian future of entire nations. For two thousand years countless Christian martyrs have poured out their blood and sacrificed their lives. Within Christendom itself, in the course of centuries, there have been many dissensions, quarrels, schisms and heresies so that today a divided Christianity is like a sixth wound in the Body of Christ. There have been the scandals, too, caused so often by those whose lives should have been models of holiness and integrity. Even today unknown is the number of those who have been baptized in the name of the Holy Trinity but are forgetful of their Christian duties and live in apathetic indifference or complete worldliness, as if supernatural realities simply do not exist.

There is more in the history of the Church, however, than darkness and shadows. There has been, and there is much that commands great admiration and sincere veneration—much goodness and progress, holiness and heroism, light of knowledge and energy of action! But the contrast between the light and the dark, between loftiness and baseness has created a painful problem, evoked objections from others and made agonizing difficulties for Christians themselves. It is a disquieting, a vexing and superhuman problem.

Pope John, from his long experience in the Middle East, in France, in Italy and elsewhere, knew this problem well and through the inspiration of the Holy Spirit he made an heroic effort to solve it. He summoned an Ecumenical Council, the twenty-first in the long history of the Church. He invited all the bishops of the world to be present and to speak their minds freely. He also invited "observers" from among our "Separated Brethren." It was the first time in history that such an invitation had been extended. Prior to the opening of the Council, throughout its entire first session and until the very hour of his death, he constantly repeated the prayer of Christ: "Ut Unum Sint"—"That all may be one."

To heal the wounds of a divided Christendom, to initiate an inner renewal of the Church in all its beauty and to further the cause of Christian unity and the unity of brotherhood among all men—these were some of the objectives of the Second Vatican Council, the supreme accomplishment of the pontificate of John XXIII. They required a Pontiff endowed with natural and supernatural qualities who would appeal to mankind and be acceptable as a Builder of Bridges between people of all faiths and all countries. John XXIII was such a Pontiff. He built a bridge between Catholic Christians and Protestant Christians, another between Christians of the West and those of the East, and a third between Christians and non-Christians. It was a bridge of respect for the conscientious religious convictions of all peoples, of mutual esteem and love among all the children of God. It was a bridge that bypassed a long, dark atmosphere of distrust and misunderstanding, a bridge built on understanding and friendship that reached the goal of dialogues and colloquia among scholars and brotherly love among people of all faiths, of no faith and of every class. The formula on which he based all the planning and specification for the bridge building program is found in his own words: "I have tried to preserve my calm and balance while investigating and evaluating things and persons about me, ever concerned more with that which unites than that which divides."

Over those bridges came great religious leaders to confer with John XXIII and powerful political leaders who had no place for religion in their governments. They were followed by the little people of all nations who wished to hear the gospel of love first preached by Christ and now expressed in modern terms by the man whom Catholics called His Vicar on earth.

The obstacles to unity among Christians are most formidable. They cannot be overcome in a short time for they have been accumulating for centuries. But they never dismayed nor discouraged Pope John and they must not defeat or prevent us from seeking one of the objectives for which he summoned Vatican Council II: "Ut Unum Sint"—"That all may be one." On the contrary, these insurmountable obstacles should stir us to more confident prayer in the faith which Our Blessed Lord said can move mountains: "I promise you, if you have faith, though it be but like a grain of mustard seed, you have only to say to this mountain, remove from this place to that, and it will remove; nothing will be impossible for you."

"This heart-breaking problem of the disunity of Christ's heritage," said Pope John, "remains to the prejudice and hindrance of our best efforts, and the way ahead is paved with difficulties and doubts." But the peace of the world depends upon this unity, and therefore upon how we work and how we pray to bring it about. We should not lose courage but "continue," as Pope John recommended, "to extend a loving invitation to our separated brothers, who like us bear the name of Christ, read His holy Gospel and who listen also to the promptings of religious piety and of a charity that blesses and benefits."

The mountainous obstacles confronting unity among Christians may not be moved for many generations, but we can perpetuate our love for and remembrance of the beloved bridge builder, Pope John XXIII by maintaining the bridges he has built between all peoples so that the day will be hastened when the prayer of our Lord at the Last Supper will be answered—"Holy Father, keep them true to Thy name, Thy gift to me, that they may be one as we are one. . . . That they all may be one. . . .That they, too, may be one in us as Thou, Father, art in me and I in Thee."

The Ecumenical Council—to be known in history as Vatican Council II—was undoubtedly the supreme accomplishment of Pope John during his brief pontificate. If he had lived until October 28, 1963, he would have reigned for only five years. Many there were who expected from this aging and ailing man a short interim term, an interregnum and "caretaker" regime. They were correct in their prediction that his pontificate would be short; they were wrong in predicting that it would have the character of a "caretaker." So many new accomplishments were crowded into four and a half years by the late Pope that it would be impossible to describe them all.

He increased the number of Cardinals above seventy for the first time in four centuries and included a Cardinal from Africa and Japan. He lifted the Catholic Church from its moorings of past ages into the bewildering chaos of the twentieth century. For the first time in four hundred years he established a department within the Vatican for better relations between all Christians and called it the Secretariate for the Promotion of Christian Unity which he described as a "special sign of esteem and affection for separated Christians." Its function would be to enable them to follow the work of the Council as closely as possible. As head of the Secretariate, the Pope appointed Augustine Cardinal Bea, a surprising appointment in the opinion of many. Cardinal Bea was well known as a biblical scholar. Some knew him as an extraordinary spiritual director and the confessor of two Popes. Few were prepared to see him in his late seventies emerge on the international plane in a totally new role.

For the first time in the history of Ecumenical Councils, Pope John invited representatives of other religions to be present as observers at the Second Vatican Council and afforded them every possible courtesy and opportunity to see at close range the entire proceedings of every meeting of the first session. Prior to the opening of this Council, he sent Vatican observers to the third assembly of the World Council of Churches in New Delhi in 1961 and he planned, before his death, to send similar observers to the fourth assembly of the Lutheran World Federation.

He sponsored new contacts with communistic nations and individual communistic governments in the hope of advancing the cause of world peace. He published eight encyclicals, of which "PACEM IN TERRIS" —"Peace on Earth" and "MATER ET MAGISTRA"— "Mother and Teacher" are best known. The former was addressed to all men of good will; the latter was an eloquent appeal for world peace. He shattered precedent after precedent as he travelled on foot, by train or automobile at least one hundred times outside the territorial limits of Vatican City. Those in hospitals, prisons, orphan asylums and homes for the aged, those living in slums and along the highways, frequently saw this man of God going about doing good.

"Be ye perfect," said the Lord, "as your Heavenly Father is perfect." If we would attempt to look with prying eyes into the inner life of Good Pope John XXIII we might say that its scaffolding was like a ladder. On the lowest step thereof was the virtue of humility; on the highest—charity, union with God. In between we would place on the other steps of that ladder all the beautiful qualities of kindness, gentleness, friendliness, love of neighbor, courage, vision, intimacy with God, and other virtues so evident in the character of this man of God who was able to surmount every barrier, to dissolve many ancient prejudices and capture not merely the imaginations, but the hearts of men everywhere.

Pope John XXIII completed the long climb up the ladder of perfection. He reached the summit of charity and is united with God. His epitaph can best be written by those of us who imitate those qualities of soul which he preached and practiced. We can make his memory live among us, just as surely as he continues to live with the Father in heaven, by reflecting in our lives those virtues which shone so mightily and so beautifully in his life. Though a man of advanced years when he was elected to the papacy, he was young at heart in every way, seeing the world in freshness and simplicity, in open-hearted candor and wondrous optimism. He was an example for our age, and though he has passed from among us, that example will linger on and glow more brilliantly with the passing of time. Good Pope John has gone to his reward, but his goodness will live forever.

May this great Pontiff, this greatest Builder of Spiritual Bridges in the history of Christianity, intercede for us before the throne of the Divine Architect of the world, under Whom we must all be united if we are to build a society where all men may live together in lasting peace and mutual love.

UNIVERSAL FATHER AND FRIEND

In the memory of John XXIII is traced the image of a man who was "naturally supernatural and supernaturally natural." He was mankind's Universal Father and Friend. All men were his children in God; the whole world was his diocese. His fatherly concern was never restricted to any one part of the human family. Pope John once revealed that when he said the Rosary he offered each decade for a different part of the world: Europe, Asia, America, Africa and Oceania.

There is little that words can add to the examples and deeds of this "humble servant." His faith, simple and sincere, sustained him in the face of trials and doubts. That same faith inspired his universal love; his love in turn nourished his faith.

"All this fuss and bother they are making over me does not even touch me," Pope John confided to his confessor, Father Cavagna. In the midst of the praises for "Pacem in Terris" and the Balzan Peace Prize dissenting voices raised sharp criticisms. John XXIII's only comment was: "They are in good faith. I pray for them and love them more than all the rest. I also have the good fortune of being able to forget such things quickly." His charity was all-embracing: "Let us seek that which unites, not that which divides. Let us look for what is good in others, not for what is bad." Pope John's whole outlook was colored by a vibrant optimism which constantly reminded him of the good to be found in every age and discovery of man, in every culture and civilization.

To his prodigal children fallen into the mire of sin and vice he offered mercy and loving pardon. To our Christian brethren separated from the Flock of Peter he opened wide his arms, urging the study of the path to reunion. His motu proprio establishing the Secretariate for Promoting Christian Unity has been described as the "Magna Carta of the ecumenical movement in the Church." A well-known religious leader has written that Pope John, "who won the esteem of the whole world, not through any extraordinary intellectual talent, but through the gifts of his heart, through his simplicity and humility, will go down in history not only as the Pope of the Second Vatican Council but also as the Pope of the ecumenical movement."

With the same simplicity of manner John XXIII approached the lettered and unlettered, people of world renown and the humble man of the street. In his discourses he preferred to be spontaneous, choosing words everyone could understand. He avoided any trace of oratory that did not harmonize with his gentle, unaffected manner.

It was precisely because of his desire to reach souls that John XXIII began to study English. "It is not because I just want to converse in English," he confided. "But I do not feel that I am a father to all the people I meet who speak only English, when I cannot answer them a single word." During the closing months of his Pontificate, John XXIII was often seen with a Russian grammar in his hands. Since he already spoke a little Slavic, he felt it would not be too difficult for him to master at least some Russian and in that way show his affection for that people.

John XXIII has been called the Pope who delivered humanity from the slavery of materialism, and led men across the modern Red Sea of indifferentism to the Promised Land of Faith and Love. He was possessed by an unshakable confidence in the fundamental goodness of every man and acted on this assumption. He himself was such an exemplar of benign goodness that everyone who came in contact with him felt irresistibly drawn to a higher plane of life. On hearing that "Good Pope John" was dying, even atheists asked if they could pray for him and bent their knees in humble supplication—

proof positive that the warmth of this Loving Shepherd melted even the hardened shell of disbelief.

Jean Guitton, a professor of the University of Paris and the only Catholic layman to attend the first session of Vatican II, described Pope John as a perfect blend of magnetic good-heartedness and generosity. "I often wondered how he conquered the hearts of so many people. Perhaps it was because people saw Pope John as a model they could imitate."

"My own poor person is worth nothing. It is your brother who is speaking to you, your brother who has become a Father through the Will of Our Lord Jesus Christ. Let us continue to love one another, holding fast to that which unites and leaving aside that which drives asunder," said Pope John. He felt at home anywhere, like a "member of the family." He was the Shepherd dressed in white who guided the world's five million Catholics, every one of whom could call him "Father."

During a Lenten visit to a parish church in Rome, Pope John told his "parishioners" that he took great delight in the sight of so many children carried in the arms of their parents who had come to greet the Vicar of Christ and receive his blessing.

Wherever Pope John went on his Lenten visits about Rome, that section of the city, no matter how run down and poor, was miraculously transformed in a colorful array of festive decorations. His route was jammed with applauding crowds which all but brought his black Mercedes to a halt. Even within the church there were explosions of cheers and applause at the sight of "Papa Giovanni."

"These visits outside the Vatican to the parishes of my diocese," he told his parishioners, "give us great consolation. The Pope is a hermit in a large palace. The whole world comes to see him but just the same, he is a hermit living in a few small rooms. Let the Pope come out for a little while, at least during Lent, to give you some good inspirations and we can encourage one another in our daily sacrifices."

A large placard reading, "We give our hearts to the Pope" greeted him on one of his final trips outside the Vatican. The people, his people—the fathers and mothers of families, children, workers, the young and the old—instinctively penetrated the essence of the pontificate of John XXIII: his priestly heart.

"It is the Pope's care and joy to bring everyone the happiness of the grace of God"—everyone, even the forgotten: the inmates of Regina Coeli Prison, hospitalized children, delinquent boys. "The Pope is a priest. He is the highest and first among priests and must give good example and carry his cross." "Since I was a boy, I never thought of anything else except being a priest."

"To think," Archbishop Roncalli said on learning of his elevation to the Cardinalate, "that I would have so much loved to be a parish priest, or at least to finish as a Bishop in some out-of-the-way diocese." This pastoral instinct colored every aspect of the five-year pontificate in which Pope John XXIII was the "pastor of the world."

The stories and anecdotes which sparkle through these years serve but to highlight the details of an already well-drawn portrait.

Leaving the conclave immediately after his election, Pope John XXIII found his secretary, Msgr. Loris Capovilla in tears. "Oh, Monsignor," he said, "who is the new Pope, you or me?" "But what are we going to do now?" was the reply. "Say Vespers and Compline as usual," answered Pope John.

A few days after his election, Pope John made it quite clear that his three brothers, his sister and ten nephews were not to be called, "Their Excellencies, the Relatives of His Holiness." "How are we to call them, Holy Father?" he was asked. "Just say: the family of John XXIII."

In one of his earliest audiences, John XXIII candidly confessed, "Now I am making my novitiate as Pope. Help me." Rarely, even in the final months of his pontificate would he remember to use the majestic plural, "We." Occasionally he remembered to use it at the beginning of a discourse but soon reverted to the singular "I".

John XXIII once related that in the first days of his pontificate he would often awake with a start in the middle of the night, his head swimming with troubled thoughts and grave problems. "I will have to talk to the Holy Father about these. He will know just what to do." After a few moments, he would come back to reality: "But I am the Pope!" With a gentle sigh he concluded, "Well, if I am the Pope I will have to talk to the good God about them."

To a group of pilgrims from Venice and Bergamo Pope John confided his impressions of his first trip in the "Sedia Gestatoria," the portable papal throne carried on the shoulders of eight papal servants. It made him think, he told them, of when he was a little boy and his mother or father carried him on their shoulders. He concluded, "The secret of success in all things is to let oneself be carried by our Lord and to carry our Lord everywhere." Actually, John XXIII reserved the use of the "Sedia Gestatoria" for solemn functions when he had no other choice but to use it. "That rocking back and forth makes me seasick!" he joked.

Cold formality and rigid protocol were two things directly opposed to the simplicity of John XXIII. Vatican tradition, for instance, dictated that the Pope had to dine alone. Not finding anything in the Gospels to support this tradition, Pope John began inviting Bishops and Cardinals to dinner. "Let us go and have a bite to eat," he would say to his surprised guests without making any special fuss.

Pope John took great joy in consoling the sick and suffering. He often went unannounced to the bedside of an ailing priest or dying prelate. During an audience for the sick and crippled he lovingly told them, "They say that when a person grows old he has a second childhood. Isn't that wonderful–to become children again! If we do not become like little children, imitating their simplicity, it is more difficult to enter the Kingdom of Heaven."

One day in the spring of 1961 a wheelchair was brought into the Small Throne Room in the Vatican. A little girl dressed in white got up from the wheelchair and with unsteady steps walked toward the white figure, smilingly looking at her. Pope John and little Katherine Hudson who was dying of lukemia, passed precious moments in affectionate conversation. With difficulty Pope

John held back his tears. Katherine was radiant with joy. It seemed almost as if she wanted to console the Pope. Close to her heart she held the cherished gifts he gave her: a beautiful Rosary, a medal and an autographed picture of himself.

When it was time to leave, Pope John stood up and stretched out his arms toward that little girl so close to death. "My child," he whispered, "pray for me."

Pope John's last general audience was held in St. Peter's on May 15, 1963. He spoke to the throngs gathered about him of the eternal youth of the Church. "We are not gathered here next to the Tomb of the Apostle for a funeral. But even so, funerals are times of joy, too. . . . Oh, the Hail Mary, the Hail Mary! The first Hail Mary of the child; the last Hail Mary of the dying man. . . ."

The festive crowd did not understand. Those who knew beheld a joyous smile on that face already lined by pain and sickness. Carried in the "Sedia Gestatoria" Pope John moved away, a figure of almost unearthly whiteness, a Father ceaselessly blessing his beloved children.

THE GREAT HEART

OF POPE JOHN

Over a period of more than thirty years Pope John revealed in his diary some beautiful thoughts that welled up in his great heart. From this we have taken a few that may be a source of meditation to many.

Today is the third anniversary of my episcopal consecration. I feel myself in God's hands, near the Heart of our Lord. I seek nothing else except His glory, that of His Church, and the well being of souls in union with the Holy Father who sent me to this nation (Bulgaria).

I have no worries or desires for the future: *Thy kingdom come, Thy Will be done....* That is all.

I love my cross and bless it. My Lord Jesus, I repeat what I said to You on the day of my consecration: *May Your cross ever be my glory.*

My life must be like incense. Cast on the fire it burns and permeates the temple of the Lord with a scent of delightful sweetness.

St. Joseph, intercede for me.

1928

My vacation is over and I am back to work. The celebrations for my priestly jubilee have come to an end.

I have left so much undone here at Sofia and at Sotto il Monte. I am ashamed of myself. How many priests have worked wonders for the apostolate and the salvation of souls in twenty-five years of priesthood. And, I, what have I done?

My Jesus, mercy!

Humiliating myself for the little or nothing I have accomplished until now, I raise my eyes to the future. There is still light before me, still hope for good. Once again I take up my staff, which soon will be that of an old man, and go forth to meet all that our Lord will ask of me.

I was so discouraged last July that I was tempted to beg the Holy Father to relieve me of the burden of this apostolic Visitation. Those were moments of weakness. I must and shall remain where obedience has placed me until the end.

Now, after all the celebrations, the comforting words of the Holy Father and my vacation during which I enjoyed the delights of the pastoral ministry among my good people of Bergamo, I feel myself more than ever ready to follow my path calmly and serenely, no matter what the cost or condition. I do not want, think or dream of anything else in the world for myself except doing my duty day by day, for the love and glory of Jesus my Lord and for His Holy Church.

1929

Today I am fifty years old. I want to sanctify this event by an evening vigil of solitary, intimate prayer.

My Jesus, on Your part these are fifty years of grace but on my part, years full of imperfections and faults. I bless You, I praise You. I have nothing to offer You except my small sacrifices here in this land I love so much and would like to see enkindled with love for You, resplendent with the light of the Catholic Church, Mother and Teacher of civilization.

What are my sacrifices compared with the peace of heart You continually bestow on me and my active desire to see You loved and blessed in this land—that desire which burns and sears within me, at the same time continually giving me cause to rejoice?

What are my petty sacrifices, especially my putting up with the faults of those souls in whom I am trying my best to make charity reign; what are they when I consider my faults, negligences and sins for which I deserve every torment and suffering?

My Jesus, I accept everything from Your hands, from Your Heart. To You I say: let me suffer even more if You so will it, to purify my soul and make it a better instrument for the greater good of souls, for Your greater honor and glory and that of Holy Mother Church.

I would like at this time to ask You for a very special grace: that You preserve my beloved parents in good health.

They are so humble and unassuming, yet at the same time so rich in faith, fear of the Lord and love for the things of the spirit. Oh, continue to bless them, to comfort them and grant them, in their simple social position and in the midst of their little sorrows, a spiritual foretaste of heavenly bliss.

My future? I do not think about it. Many take a very superficial interest in what awaits me: if I am destined for the See of Milan, Turin or somewhere else. I do not think about it and I believe His Holiness would never even consider me for such important positions, so far beyond my nothingness. So I continue to live in peace and calm. O Lord, grant me the grace ever to live thus.

As for my future, once again I repeat from the bottom of my heart: *May Your Cross ever be my glory.* So may it be until the hour of my death which I am ever ready for, now or later. Amen.

O Mary, I am always yours. My Mother and my Hope!

St. Joseph, my dearest patron, intercede for me.

1930

Here we are on the threshold of a second half-century of life. This morning after Mass I reflected that our Lord might well grant me this new half-century. Oh, how I would like it to be spent all for His glory and for the triumph of His love over the earth.

Enough! Even when it comes to the question of a long or short life I leave myself in the hands of our Lord. I ask not one day more or less than has been decreed by Heaven. Of Jesus Crucified I beg: *Turn not Thy face away from me.*

These last few months have been gladdened by the nomination of the Apostolic Delegate and the successful establishment of the Delegation at Sofia. Thus seven years of patience and expectation have come to an end and a new epoch opens. We must have confidence in Our Lord. He makes us wait but He always answers. Hence, be ever courageous and ever joyful. *The charity of God and the patience of Christ*—how I love these words.   1931

I am still in Sofia, celebrating my birthday in *solitude* and *hope.*

I want to continue trying to remain quiet and serene at my post. I have both said and written that I am not worthy to occupy the thoughts of the Holy Father. Here I am and here I shall remain, no matter what the cost. That other self within me, even though he is bound fast, would like me to feel sorry for myself. Breaking his fetters, he would like to cry out. But he will remain there, in his prison, *until death and beyond*. I will hold on high my unsullied banner with its motto: *Oboedientia et Pax*.

However, in this study of the most perfect abandonment to the holy Will of God, I feel the need of His grace. In this abandonment I discover so much sweetness and strength.

O Jesus, sustain me thus on Your breast, near Your cross until I may drink abundantly of those life-giving waters in the joys of eternal life.   1933

Patience and calm: what beautiful qualities.

◈

All is beautified by the smile of Mary, who looks with a mother's love on our humble deeds.

◈

I am commanded by obedience: I go voluntarily and with confidence.

◈

I prefer to wait, trusting that Our Lord will give us His good spirit. Certainly one must listen to both sides before forming a definite judgment.

◈

Order and charity are what matter the most.

It is Our Lord Who speaks to hearts and it is He Who moves them.

◈

The conversion of a people is a mystery of the Lord. Study, work, suffer and pray much.

◈

The little thorns that we bear for love of Jesus become roses. Calm and patience. . . .

Courtesy is a branch of charity.

◈

One must make oneself loved to be able to impose order, peace, and religious progress.

◈

Work and suffer: only in this way will one merit true rest in heaven.

◈

The good health that Our Lord continues to grant me is a grace that I in no way merit and obliges me to be more perfect in His service.

◈

Only the Lord is good and generous in His rewards.

◈

Where charity is lacking, what can we expect? O Lord, grant us a share in Your spirit.

◈

My desire for the greatest good for these souls (the Turks) preoccupies my mind, making me both happy and sad.

◈

Once a decision is made in obedience, it becomes always dearer and more pleasing to me. *Oboedientia et Pax.* Here is a new and beautiful opportunity . . . (his immediate return to Athens).

◈

What matters to me is the effort of finding a little of the good side.

◈

We must, in the care of souls, make the effort to approach, rather, to penetrate the spirit with which Jesus cares for souls. And surely the Spirit of Jesus with regard to them is more charitable than ours.

◈

I do not lack the joy of knowing that I have acted in the spirit of obedience and peace.

❖

God wants each one of us to carry his own cross, and sanctify himself on the one He has given him.

❖

It is well to feel the burden of weariness. This is due to our sins. But it is also a means of imploring grace for the souls in our care.

❖

I desire that Our Lord sustain and preserve my poor life in the service of the Holy Roman Church until my last breath.

❖

True strength lies in the generous, patient, paternal goodness of the Bishop.

❖

Our duty is to pray, to sanctify and to hope.

I am gladdened by the thought of never having cut myself off from obedience–the bearer of interior peace and success.

❖

Lord, I humble myself and offer you this sacrifice– *Oboedientia et Pax.*

❖

Today I prayed to St. Andrew that he may make love for the cross ever sweeter to me.   1938

❖

Prayer is more powerful if accompanied by penance.

❖

Even if I do nothing else, the merit of good example will never go lost.

❖

How we need to imitate the Lord and be patient with men.

❖

This is my real life: the altar, prayer, teaching and everything which promotes piety.

To be always busy but never upset by haste is a foretaste of heaven on earth. Outside of the Will of God nothing interests me.

◈

One must sweeten, restrain and direct all toward the good.

◈

Each day, like each month, comes from the hands of God. They are all, therefore, equally beautiful.

◈

A Bishop is always a public fountain.

◈

Nothing but the thought of Heaven consoles me for the death of my mother. These are the holiest days for a Christian family.

◈

It is well to let oneself be ground up by pain and by death so as to rise again.

◈

Visiting the sick is a work of mercy that always benefits souls.

◈

I prefer to continue my effort to be quiet without bitterness, sure that this mortification will prove edifying in its own time.

◈

When the roots are good, the tree will be strong and healthy even if it grows in stony ground.

◈

Let us attach ourselves to what is really worthwhile, that is, souls, the work of grace in them, conformity to the spirit of the Gospels, intimate union with Jesus and His Church.

◈

Wanting to remain ever faithful to my motto— *Oboedientia et Pax*—on the fifteenth anniversary of my arrival here in the East, I find reason for consolation, peace and even courage, thinking of nothing else except to do well what I must do, where I must do it.

All know how to suggest and more than a few how to criticize, but to direct oneself to a useful and simple service: this is something else.

◈

This search for classical and Byzantine culture is an ornament of my sacred ministry. Putting Jesus in the center, everything is brightened and enriched.

◈

O Lord, preserve my calm and interior peace amid so many little upsets.

◈

Our true rest will be in Heaven. Oh, Heaven, Heaven!   ◈

To bear these little sufferings in peace is already a sign of grace.   ◈

The light of charity and peace has to be carried everywhere.   ◈

I feel that the Lord renews and rejoices my youth. Oh, that He help me to sanctify myself. I still have time but I must not waste it.

◈

Mary, my glorious Mother, protect me always. I am your son; I am your Bishop. I love you with all my heart in Jesus and in His Church.

◈

The Lord sees all and provides for His elect.

◈

Oboedientia et Pax: this costs but it means merit for Heaven. My conscience is at peace. What need have I to worry?   ◈

It is of great comfort to feel oneself understood, followed and loved. All this happens in a form superior to my merits.

In the evening at Sotto il Monte my brothers come to keep me company and this is dearer to me than the company of princes.

◈

. . . In the most intimate conversations with the Lord, I must always understand that these are the most precious moments of my life.

◈

What more can I wish for in life? Nothing, beyond a greater effort toward perfection in living and achieving my obligation as bishop and as a servant of Holy Church. Sometimes I am stung also by poverty, that which renders me impotent to help my own who, so numerous in the house, suffer the lack of so many things. Blessed are the poor in spirit. . . .

◈

I am invited to go down to Rome as soon as possible. It was already my thought to go there after Christmas. I am happy that now obedience has been added to my action.

1939

How much light to cast on so many souls!

◈

I bought furniture for the delegation. I used money which was my own and spent it for things that will not be mine but the Church's. It seems to me a good way of fending off thoughts of avarice.

◈

To my poor fountain come men of every type. My function is to give water to all. Leaving a good impression even on the heart of a scamp seems to me a good act of charity that in its own time will bring blessings.

Human love cut off from God leads to every excess and ends in sadness. When the love of God is missing, there is little hope.

◈

The war news is always grave. It will be a slaughter which will be a great expiation for all. But for so many mothers, wives and innocent creatures, O what sorrow, what sorrow!

◈

War is a hard lesson for everyone.

◈

War is an enormous danger. For a Christian who believes in Jesus and His Gospel, it is an iniquity and a contradiction. I think that as of today, my responsibility and my duty toward wisdom, moderation and charity become more grave. I must be the Bishop of all, that is, the consul of God, the father, the beacon of encouragement for all. Nature makes me desire the success of my dear country. Grace inspires me more than ever toward proposals and efforts for peace.

◈

A good rule for me is to give all and expect nothing in return.

◈

Everything serves to demonstrate that in the sense of true peace in the world either there will be the Gospel or we will return to blood.

◈

Spiritual calm in the face of difficulties is my strength.

◈

Each day brings its own small worries. We must keep discipline of spirit, restrain impatience and maintain spiritual peace.

The thought of death follows and comforts us. Around it cluster the dearest memories of my childhood, youth and the most important events of my life.

◈

These souls need charity and unity. Instead the war will only indispose them and lead them further apart.

◈

The Holy Mass well celebrated spreads a fragrance throughout the entire day.

◈

A cross beckons to me. Lord Jesus, help me to carry it humbly and worthily.

◈

Let us act well before God; nothing else counts.

◈

I like so much to be charitable to others, while I see the Lord bestows so much of it on me.   1940

The mystery of our life is in God's hands. What matters is to walk in justice and sanctity before Heaven and our own conscience, sincere and charitable in every act.

◈

For the man who keeps his gaze confidently fixed on God there are no surprises: not even death comes as a surprise.

◈

Death is sacred because it is the gateway to glory and never-ending joy.

◈

Summary of the great graces received by one who has little esteem of himself but received good inspirations and applied them in humility and faith.

First grace — To accept the honor and weight of the pontificate with simplicity and with the joy of being able to say that I did nothing to seek it, truly nothing; that with studied and knowing care on my part not a thing was done to call any attention to my person.

Second grace — Let there come to me without complexity, simple, immediately executable ideas, which are of great import and responsibility with regard to the future. What beautiful expressions these are: to receive the good inspirations of the Lord.

1958

Let there not be factions or divisions; we all live beneath one sky, all Catholics in one world. The Divine Founder of the Church wants and intends this to be so. For this He prayed in His final hours of sacrifice. O Father, this I beg of you: *Ut unum sint*. The principle of unity among all the Churches is that sacred bond which assures them of perpetuity, of the heritage of Christ through the centuries. Let us all stand united in the Lord together with the first apostle: *With Peter to battle and with Peter to reign*.

By eliminating anything which from a human point of view might impede a more rapid advance, we present the Church in all her splendor 'without blemish and without wrinkle' and say to our separated brethren: See brothers, this is the Church of Christ. We strive our utmost to be faithful and ask Our Lord for the grace that the Church remain ever as He willed her to be.

1959

The tongue that praises God, together with all the voices of the universe, must be constantly at the service of fraternal charity. It should be used to affirm the good. As for evil, it must not hide or deny it, but pity those who are guilty and work for the conversion of the erring. We would be far more successful in many things if our use of the tongue were better directed and regulated.

◇

The humble successor of St. Peter has not yet had any temptation to discouragement. We feel strong in faith and with Jesus at our side we can cross not only the tiny sea of Galilee but all the seas of the world. The Word of Jesus is sufficient for salvation and victory.

1960

A well prepared Confession made weekly on Friday or Saturday is the solid foundation upon which to work out one's sanctification. This practice keeps one ready to die a good death at any hour and moment of the day. My calm and readiness to leave and present myself to the Lord at any instant seems to me such a pledge of trust and love as to merit from that Jesus, Whose Vicar on earth I am, an abundance of His mercy.

Let us always proceed toward Him as He awaits me with open arms.

To strengthen my habitual confidence I like to quote Rosmini's remembrance of the admirable Father Caraffa, seventh Superior General of the Society of

Jesus. He was always occupied in meditating on three very familiar letters: one *black,* one *crimson* and one *white.* The *black* letter stood for his sins; the *crimson* for the Passion of our Savior, Jesus; the *white* for the glory of the blessed in Heaven.

These three images surely sum up the fruit of good Christian meditation.

The *black* letter helps me know myself and urges me to purify my soul. The *crimson* letter familiarizes me with the Passion of Jesus, Who suffers in body and in spirit. The *white* letter urges me to combat discouragement, desolation and sadness, while all the Saints continue to encourage me to suffer bravely, reminding me that our present light affliction is *not worthy to be compared with the future glory that will be revealed in us.*

◈

I want this retreat to mark real progress in the study of my personal sanctification: not only as a Christian, priest and Bishop, but as Pope—as the *good Father of all Christians,* as the *Good Shepherd* which the Lord has willed to make me, notwithstanding how small and unworthy I am.

Many times I reflect on the mystery of the Precious Blood of Jesus, the devotion which as Pope I felt immediately inspired to spread to complement the devotions to the *Name* and *Heart* of Jesus which are, as they say, well known and fairly widespread.

I must confess it was an unexpected inspiration for me. The private devotion to the Precious Blood I saw practiced by my Great Uncle Zaverio. He was the eldest of the five Roncalli brothers. In fact, he was my first guide in those religious practices out of which my priestly vocation rapidly, almost spontaneously, developed. I remember the devotional books he kept on his kneeler. Among them was "The Precious Blood" which he used during the month of July. Oh sacred and blessed memories of my boyhood! How they come back, precious in the twilight of the eventide of my life, highlighting the foundations of my sanctification and granting me a consoling glimpse of what awaits me—I humbly trust—in eternity.

The Crucifix and eternity—the Passion of Jesus in the endless light of eternity: Oh what sweetness and it will ever be so! The life that still remains for me on earth must be penetrated through and through by peace, spent at the foot of the cross of Jesus Crucified, cleansed by His Precious Blood and the tears of the Sorrowful Virgin, the Mother of Jesus and my Mother.

This impulse which has lately overtaken me is like a new spirit, a voice that infuses generosity and burning fervor in my heart which I love to manifest in three distinct ways:

1) A complete detachment from all things; hence a perfect indifference toward criticism as well as praise and toward anything that may befall me in this world;

2) In front of the Lord I am dust, a sinner: I live through the mercy of Jesus to which I owe all and from which I expect all. I submit myself to Him even to the point of letting myself be completely transformed by His sorrows and sufferings in the fullest abandonment of absolute conformity to His Will. Now more than ever, as long as I shall live, and in all things: *Oboedientia et Pax;*

3) A readiness to live or to die, as St. Peter and St. Paul and to face anything, even chains, sufferings, anathema or martyrdom for Holy Mother Church and the souls redeemed by Jesus. I feel the weight of my office and I tremble, knowing myself to be weak and frail. But I place my trust in Christ Crucified and His Mother and look toward eternity.

◈

Treat everyone with respect, prudence and the simplicity recommended in the Gospels.

Simplicity never contradicts prudence nor vice versa. Simplicity is love; prudence is thought. Love prays; the intellect watches. *"Watch and pray...."*—a perfect blend. Love is like the dove that murmurs. The intellect is like the serpent that never falls to the ground nor hurts himself because he foresees all the rough spots in his path.

◈

Jesus Christ is the Founder of the Church. He guides every event according to His own good pleasure with wisdom, power and unerring goodness for the greater benefit of His elect who are the members of His Mystical Spouse.

Though circumstances may appear contrary to the good of the Church, I must remain perfectly calm. This however, does not dispense me from hoping and praying that God's Will be done, *on earth as it is in Heaven.*

I must guard against the audacity of those fools who, intellectually blind or tricked by hidden pride, presume to do great things in the Church without having been called by God—as if our Divine Redeemer had need of their miserable cooperation, or that of any man.

What really matters is to cooperate with God for the good of souls and the whole world. This is the highest expression of the office of the Pope.

"In all things look to your end." We are not dealing merely with the end of human life, but with the *divine vocation* to which the Pope is raised by the mysterious dispositions of Divine Providence.

This vocation finds its expression in a triple splendor: the *personal sanctity* of the Pope which makes his life glorious; love for the *Holy, Universal Church* according to that measure of divine grace which alone can prepare and assure *final glory*. Jesus Christ alone directs and governs the Church according to His good pleasure through the Pope, in the light of that same glory which is the highest on earth and in eternity.

The sacred duty of the humble Pope is to purify all his intentions in the light of this glory, living in conformity with this doctrine and grace, so as to merit the great honor of being similar in perfection to Christ, whose Vicar he is—with Christ Crucified, at the price of His Blood, Redeemer of the world; with Christ Rabbi, Master, the One true Teacher of all ages and people.

Be satisfied with your daily apostolate; don't lose time in trying to foretell the future.

Christ yesterday and today, now and forever.

Not to make prophecies or give any guarantees for the future is the *rule of conduct* based on that spirit of calmness and fortitude through which the faithful and my co-workers must receive light and encouragement from the Pope as the first Priest.

It suffices to take care of the present. To put our fantasy and anxiety to work constructing the future is a waste of time. The Vicar of Christ knows what Christ wants of him. Others do not have to give him advice or suggest undertakings to him. The fundamental rule of conduct for the Pope is to be always content with his present state and not to worry about the future, to accept all from the hands of the Lord without human reservation, and refrain from speaking about the future with any assurance or certainty, no matter with whom it might be.

The experiences of these three years of my pontifical service which, *tremens et timens,* I accepted out of pure obedience to the will of the Lord expressed by the voice of the Sacred College of Cardinals in Conclave, bear witness to and unfailingly motivate me to fidelity to this maxim: absolute abandonment in God as regards the present and perfect calm about the future.

The various undertakings of a pastoral character which are woven through this first part of my pontificate have all come from the calm and loving—I might almost say silent—inspiration of Our Lord to his poor servant, who without any merit of his own, except that of simply not objecting but agreeing and obeying, has been a useful instrument for the honor of Jesus and the edification of countless souls.

My first contacts with the great and with the lowly, a charitable visit here and there, meekness and humility of manner, clarity of ideas, fervent encouragement, Lenten visits to new parishes, the overwhelming success of the Diocesan Synod of Rome, the naming of numerous Cardinals and Bishops of every nation, race and color, and now the powerful and world-wide Ecumenical Movement–all these confirm the worth of the principle of awaiting the good inspirations of Jesus and carrying them out with faith, modesty and fervent confidence. Jesus presides over the government of the world leading it to the sublime ends of creation: the redemption and eternal glorification of souls.

◈

I notice in my body the beginning of some trouble which must be natural for an old man. I bear it in peace, though it annoys me sometimes and because it causes me to fear that it is becoming worse. It is not pleasant to think of it too much, but once again I am ready for everything.

◈

This bed is an altar. The altar needs a victim. Behold me ready. I have before me a clear vision of my soul, of my priesthood, of the Council and the Universal Church.

◈

I am at peace. I have always wanted the Will of God–always, always. I pray for the Church, for children, for priests and for Bishops so that they may be holy, and for the whole world. . . . Coming from poverty and the smallness of Sotto il Monte, I have sought never to forget them.

What great graces has the Lord given me: holy pastors, exemplary parents, a strong Christian tradition and contented and tranquil poverty. I wish to die knowing that I have nothing. Poverty many times distressed me, especially when I was not able to help my family or some fellow priest. But I never grieved about it.

(Among the special intentions for which he offered his Rosary, John XXIII listed:)

My Bergamo, and the dear brothers of Bulgaria, the Turks and Greeks. I see again the eight years I passed among the French, who treated me well and whom I loved and love greatly. I see again Venice, my Venice, which I have always on my lips and in my heart. And then behold me here near St. Peter's and the Lateran. In the first days of this pontifical service, I didn't realize fully what it was to be the Bishop of Rome, and by virtue of that the pastor of the universal Church. Then one week after another it emerged in full light and I felt at home, as I never felt in the whole of my life.

◈

Peace! Peace! I desire that this be the last prayer of the Pope, of the humble Pope John.

◈

We are comforted and strengthened in the security of obeying the good and mighty Will of God. This security, while a reason for peace and habitual abandonment to grace from above, also strengthens our spirit and undertakings, raising them on the wings of an expectation that trusts solely in God.   1961

⧗

During the first conversation of the morning of January 20, 1959, with my Secretary of State, there came to my lips the words ecumenical council, diocesan synod and the recasting of the Code of Canon Law, without ever having thought of them before, and contrary to every one of my thoughts and considerations on these points.

The first to be surprised by my proposal was I my-self, without it having been suggested to me by anyone. And it can be said that all appeared to me very natural in the immediate and subsequent phases.

After three years of preparation, continuous, happy and tranquil work, behold us now on the slopes of the holy mountain. May the Lord support us and bring all to a good conclusion.

◈

Yes, the Catholic Church is the architect and teacher of peace. We say it with a sure conscience. She continues in the world the mission of her Founder, Jesus Christ, Who in an eloquent prophecy was called the "Prince of Peace."

◈

Above all else, this and only this really counts: to know God, to follow His commandments, to gather the fruits of the Redemption and to walk, to walk *in justice and sanctity before His face all the days of our lives.*

◈

The Holy Catholic Church of God that wants to be a Light to all peoples, has a message for all men of our day and age. She wants to remind men of the value of the things of the spirit, to invoke the institution of a just and more noble civil and domestic order in which all the children of God redeemed by the Blood of Christ can live in mutual love, respecting even the smallest rights and duties.

◈

Having entered, and by now even left my eightieth year of age does not trouble my mind. . . . In fact it leaves me tranquil and confident. It is the usual thing: I do not desire anything more or less than the Lord continues to give me. I thank and bless Him for each single day, prepared for everything.

The exercise of the word, which must be substantial and not in vain, leads me to desire a closer approach to the writings of the great Pontiffs of ancient times. In these months I feel familiar with St. Leo the Great and Innocent III. . . .

But above all, I want to insist on saintly intimacy with the Lord: in remaining in tranquil and loving conversation with Him. . . .

O, how I feel the significance and the tenderness of the "Domine, non sum dignus" (Lord, I am not worthy) spoken every morning, with the Sacred Host in my hand and as a seal of humility and love.

◈

It seems to us that we have to disagree with certain prophets of gloom who are always foretelling grave disasters, as if the end of the world were at hand.

1962

My children, always trust in God Who watches over each one of you. Remember what the Gospel says: "Little children, love one another—this is the greatest of the Commandments."

◈

The Church is Jesus living in every century. Anchored with the mystic bark of Peter in Rome, center of Catholicism and universal magisterium. His reign is characterized by meekness, love and charity.

Pacem in Terris, what an echo! What is mine in this document is above all the humble example which I have tried to give during all my poor life.

◈

He has regarded the humility of his handmaid and therefore, also the *humility of his servant.* It is in humility that the Pope intends to act in the service of mankind and world peace. He will remain close to the teachings of the Gospel, at the same time avoiding all harshness or indulgent weakness, both of which are harmful to souls.

◈

The Council! God knows that to this great inspiration I opened my small soul with simplicity. Will He grant that I complete it? Blessed be the Lord. Will He not grant it? From heaven where I hope–I am certain– that the Divine Mercy will want to lift me, I will see its happy conclusion. . . .

◈

"True doctrine was in his mouth, and no dishonesty was found upon his lips, he walked with Me in integrity and uprightness and turned many away from evil" (Mal. 2:6). I would like this to be my funeral eulogy.

◈

Our Lord knows what I am. That is enough for me.

◈

You have loved me because you found goodness in me.

◈

I am at peace. I have always wanted the Will of God –always, always . . . .

1963

ENCYCLICAL LETTERS
AND
ADDRESSES
OF
POPE JOHN XXIII

During his brief reign of less than five years as the spiritual leader of the world's half billion Catholics, Pope John XXIII wrote eight encyclicals.

In his first encyclical, **Ad Petri Cathedram** (To the Chair of Peter) issued in June 1959, Pope John made a solemn appeal for unity among Christians and for world peace. "God created men as brothers, not as enemies. If the fires of discord are set ablaze in the world again, nothing else awaits all people but appalling destruction and ruin."

"Note, we beg of you," he wrote, "when we lovingly invite you to the unity of the Church, we are inviting you not to the home of a stranger, but to your own, to the Father's house which belongs to all."

To commemorate the centenary of the death of the Curé of Ars, St. John Vianney, Pope John issued his second encyclical in August 1959, **Sacerdotii Nostri Primordia** (In the Beginning of Our Priesthood). He hailed the humble Curé as the model for priests in today's world and encouraged Christian families "to give their children with joy and gratitude to the service of the Church."

During October 1959, the Pope issued his third encyclical, **Grata Recordatio** (Grateful Memory). He urged the faithful the world over to recite the Rosary during October for five special intentions: guidance for the Holy Father, for missionaries, for peace among nations, for the success of the Roman Synod and for the coming Ecumenical Council.

A month later, to commemorate the fortieth anniversary of Pope Benedict XV's apostolic letter on the missions, "Maximum Illud", Pope John issued his fourth encyclical, **Princeps Pastorem** (Prince of Shepherds). In this 9,000 word document, he stressed the importance of training a native clergy: "In our fatherly concern, We cherish the hope that it will be possible before long to choose priests from every nation to undertake the training and spiritual direction of students of their own nationality. And even now we urge Bishops and rectors of Catholic missions not to hesitate to select from among the local clergy, priests who are qualified by virtuous living and special aptitude to teach their own co-nationals in the seminary and guide them along the road to priestly holiness."

Mater et Magistra (Christianity and Social Progress) was issued in July 1961, on the occasion of the seventieth anniversary of Leo XIII's "Rerum Novarum", the first great social encyclical of modern times. Pope John wrote that it was the duty of the wealthy nations of the world to help under-developed peoples and end "their state of poverty, misery and hunger." Amounting to almost 25,000 words, this document was hailed by sociologists everywhere, who predicted that it would exert a profound influence on the Church's role in social and economic life. One of the most remarkable features of **Mater et Magistra** was the extraordinary stir it created among non-Catholics and its impact on the world of politics and economics. The text was frequently cited during debates in the United Nations Economic and Social Council. Excerpts were distributed by the European Economic Community and newspapers of every continent reported and commented on it.

On December 6, 1961 Pope John issued his sixth encyclical, **Aeterna Dei Sapientia** (The Eternal Wisdom of God), commemorating the fifteen-hundredth anniversary of the death of Pope St. Leo the Great who halted Attila the Hun at the gates of Rome. It was a tribute to the Pope who directed one of the earliest General Councils of the Church, the Council of Chalcedon in 415.

Pope John's seventh encyclical, **Paenitentium Agere** (Prayer and Penance), issued in July 1962, was a call to Catholics to draw down the blessings of God on the Ecumenical Council set to open in October of that year, through the fervent practice of prayer and penance.

Addressed to "all men of good will," **Pacem in Terris** (Peace on Earth), was Pope John's eighth and final encyclical. Never before in the history of the modern world had any papal document created such instantaneous and world-wide repercussions. World leaders vied with one another in hailing the 100,000 word encyclical as a document of extraordinary scope and significance and supported the Pope's call for a "personal contribution from all men for world peace, regardless of race, religion or politics."

In each of his encyclicals, discourses and addresses, John XXIII sought to bring the Church into the midst of the chaotic conditions of the twentieth century. To every problem and subject about which he wrote or spoke, he brought the gentle wisdom and benign charity that illumined his entire life.

In addition to the foregoing Encyclical Letters Pope John XXIII spoke on numerous subjects sometimes extemporaneously, sometimes from a prepared text, on a variety of subjects that concern problems of our times.

TRUTH

"Accept the invitation lovingly directed to each one of you to look within yourself. Do it with humility and trepidation, and ask yourself every night of your life if you have placed mind, imagination, tongue, pen and heart—your heart, above all—at the service of truth."

EVIL

"The two opposite extremes, good and evil, remain now and will remain in the future, for the will of man always will be free to express itself and able to go astray;

but the final and eternal victory in each individual chosen soul and in the chosen souls of each people will belong to Christ. . . ."

THE BROTHERHOOD OF MAN

"God created men as brothers, not foes. He gave them the earth to be cultivated by their toil and labor. Each and every man is to enjoy the fruits of the earth and receive from it his sustenance and the necessities of life. The various nations are simply communities of men, that is, of brothers. They are to work in brotherly co-operation for the common prosperity of human society, not simply for their own particular goals."

LABOR–MANAGEMENT RELATIONS

"Industrialists, managers and workers are not, and must not be, irreconcilable competitors. They are co-workers in a common undertaking that demands first of all mutual understanding and a sincere effort to overcome the temptation on each one's part to seek his own profit to the detriment of the others sharing in the common effort. It is a question of justice and a question of the application of the Christian spirit."

HUNGER

"Considering the wondrous growth of modern transportation facilities, one can no longer say that the hunger and malnutrition prevalent in certain regions are due solely to the lack of available natural resources; for these resources abound in other regions. What is lacking is intelligent and willing organization and co-ordination, capable of ensuring a fair distribution of resources. Then, too, the developing nations must be taught to make full use of their own resources."

THE BLESSING OF PEACE

"There is nothing so dear to our heart as the prosperity of peoples, their spiritual and material welfare, and we should like to see them assured particularly of the incomparable blessing to which they all aspire and which is in a certain way the prerequisite of all others: the blessing of peace.

" 'The gift of peace is so great,' said St. Augustine, 'that there is nothing more agreeable among earthly and mortal things; one cannot seek for anything more desirable, one can find nothing better.' "

SUFFERING

"Unfortunately, there are many who regard any form of physical suffering as an evil, and an absolute evil at that. They have forgotten that suffering is the inheritance of the sons of Adam. They have forgotten that the only real evil is sin, which offends God; and they have forgotten that we must look up to the cross of Jesus Christ in the same spirit in which the apostles, the martyrs, and the saints looked up to it. They taught us, and bore witness, that in the cross there is consolation and salvation, that we cannot live in the love of Christ without suffering."

HUMILITY

"Humility reduces the vision a man has of himself down its proper proportions, in accordance with right reason. The gift of fear of God follows close upon it to perfect the soul by making the Christian aware that God alone is the highest good and his own true greatness, and by bringing him to offer God the greatest reverence and to avoid sin as the one evil that can separate him from God forever. This is the key to the practical wisdom that guides the life of the wise and prudent man. 'The fear of the Lord is the beginning of wisdom,' the Sacred Book tells us."

EXPLORING OUTER SPACE

"People in general, and the young in particular, are following with enthusiasm the developments involved in these wonderful flights and trips through space. Oh, how We wish that these undertakings would take on a meaning of homage rendered to God, Creator and Supreme Lawmaker.

"Just as these historic events will take their place in the annals of the scientific knowledge of the cosmos, may they also become an expression of true and peaceful progress, contributing toward the sound foundation of human brotherhood."

THE LORD'S DAY

"The weakening of conscience with regard to the sacred character of Sunday not only has an adverse effect on public morals, but it can also pose an obstacle to the movement of grace and turn society in the direction of religious indifferentism which is regrettable and harmful. On the day of the Lord, the faithful should stop being men of the machine and earthly commotion; let them truly refrain from labor, not merely from so-called servile labor, but also from the other kind that detracts from the intellectual peace and calm necessary for our elevation to heavenly things in prayer, in active participation in liturgical life and in meditation on the word of God."

UNITY AND PEACE

"The whole world rests on these words—unity and peace—from its creation to the end of its days: that is what is meant by unity. They express the beneficent and fruitful light of the grace of Christ, Son of God, Redeemer and Glorifier of mankind: and this is what is meant by peace. The only condition required on the part of man is *good will,* which is a grace of God, but is freely conditioned upon man's response. The lack of this response of human freedom to God's call to the service of His merciful designs constitutes the most terrible problem of human history and of the lives of individual men and peoples."

MAN AND SOCIETY

"Man is composed not merely of body, but of soul as well, and is endowed with reason and freedom. Now such a composite being absolutely requires a moral law rooted in religion, which, far better than any external force or advantage, can contribute to the resolution of problems affecting the lives of individual citizens, or with a bearing upon single states or all states together.

"Whatever the progress in technology and economic life, there can be neither justice nor peace in the world, so long as men fail to realize how great is their dignity; for they have been created by God and are His children. We speak of God, Who must be regarded as the first and final cause of all things He has created".

THE UNITED NATIONS

"It is Our ardent desire that the United Nations Organization—in its structure and in its means—may become ever more equal to the magnitude and nobility of its tasks, and may the time come as quickly as possible when every human being will find therein an effective safeguard for the rights which derive directly from his dignity as a person, and which are therefore universal, inviolable and inalienable rights. This is all the more to be hoped for since all human beings, as they take an ever more active part in the public life of their own country, are showing an increasing interest in the affairs of all peoples, and are becoming more consciously aware that they are living members of the whole human family."

BLOOD DONORS

"We do not hesitate to call your service as blood donors an apostolate. Actually, it concerns the corporal and spiritual well-being of your suffering neighbor, for whom it is often the irreplaceable anchor of salvation and the stimulation to new confidence in Divine Providence. So many lives saved, so many pains alleviated, so many hopes revived for anxiously waiting families in the silence of hospitals! Yours is truly, then, an apostolate. But to achieve its perfection it must be rooted and founded in charity, which is love of God and of brothers. Just as the silent bloodstream gives life, coloring, and energy to the whole body, charity, too, hidden but pulsating, life-giving lymph, makes every good work meritorious and efficacious. Without charity acts of heroism would be like sounding brass or tinkling cymbals, with charity even a single drop of blood acquires supernatural value before God."

PRIVATE PROPERTY

"The right of private property, including that pertaining to goods devoted to productive enterprises, is permanently valid. Indeed, it is rooted in the very nature of things, whereby we learn that individual men are prior to civil society, and hence, that civil society is to be directed toward men as its end. Indeed, the right of private individuals to act freely in economic affairs is recognized in vain, unless they are at the same time given an opportunity of freely selecting and using things necessary for the exercise of this right. Moreover, experience and history testify that where political regimes do not allow private individuals the possession also of productive goods, the exercise of human liberty is violated or completely destroyed in matters of primary importance. Thus it becomes clear that in the right of property, the exercise of liberty finds both a safeguard and a stimulus."

TEACHERS

"Since your first task is to shape the minds of your pupils, keep abreast of the latest teaching techniques and develop your knowledge of your profession. A loftier task assigned to you is the shaping of student's souls. This is done by word, example and patient labor. This art cannot be learned from books but is acquired only by the grace of God, by prayer, and by living a Christian life. Educators mold tomorrow's adults by instilling in their hearts impressions which will be lifelong. By educating minds and shaping souls you are acquiring a luminous crown in Heaven. Do not let immediate problems and projects obscure the final goal in all your actions but consider all from the standpoint of eternal values. When trials, misunderstandings and fatigue threaten you, take courage from the thought of the glory

God is preparing in Heaven for His good and faithful servants."

ONE WORLD

"Today the exchange of goods and ideas, travel from one country to another, have greatly increased. Consequently, the close relations of individuals, families, intermediate associations belonging to different countries, have become vastly more frequent, and conferences between heads of states are held at shorter intervals. At the same time the interdependence of national economies has grown deeper, one becoming progressively more closely related to the other, so that they become, as it were, integral parts of the one world economy. Finally, the social progress, order, security and peace of each country are necessarily connected with the social progress, order, security and peace of all other countries.

"Given these conditions, it is obvious that individual countries cannot rightly seek their own interests and develop themselves in isolation from the rest, for the prosperity and development of one country follows partly in the train of prosperity and progress of all the rest and partly produces that prosperity and progress."

A JUST WAGE

"The remuneration of work is not something that can be left to the laws of the market place; nor should it be a decision left to the will of the more powerful. It must be determined in accordance with justice and equity; which means that workers must be paid a wage which allows them to live a truly human life and to fulfill their family obligations in a worthy manner. Other factors, too, enter into the assessment of a just wage: namely, the effective contribution which each individual

"There burns in my heart," Pope John once said to a group of non-Catholics, "the intention of working and suffering to hasten the hour when for all men the prayer of Jesus at the Last Supper will have reached its fulfillment: Ut Unum Sint— That all may be one."

Pope John was young in heart in every way, seeing the world
in freshness and simplicity, in open-hearted candor
and wondrous optimism.

The kindness, gentleness, love of neighbor, courage, vision and intimacy with God so evident in the character of John XXIII surmounted every barrier, dissolved many prejudices and captured the hearts of men everywhere.

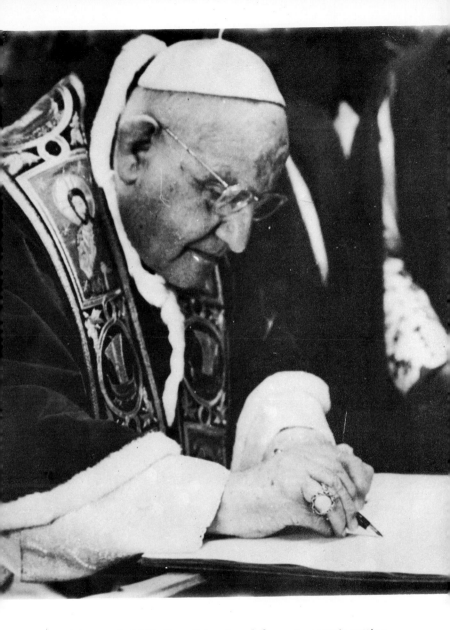

On February 2, 1962, Pope John signed the motu proprio setting
the opening date for the first session of the
Second Vatican Council.

A valiant woman—a beloved Pope.

The Holy Father on his way to the Shrine of Loretto
to beg Our Lady's intercession for the success of
the Ecumenical Council.

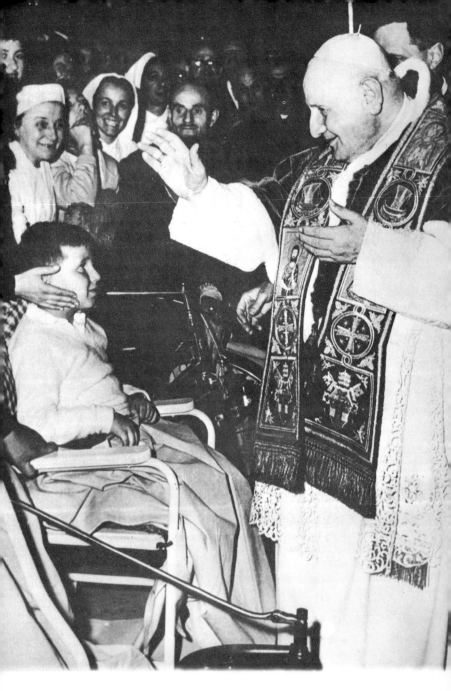

While at Loretto Pope John blessed the sick
who had come to Our Lady's shrine.

In solemn procession, over 3,000 Council Fathers entered St. Peter's Basilica for the opening of the Second Vatican Council, October 11, 1962.

Pope John receiving a group of thirty-nine non-Catholic observers at the Ecumenical

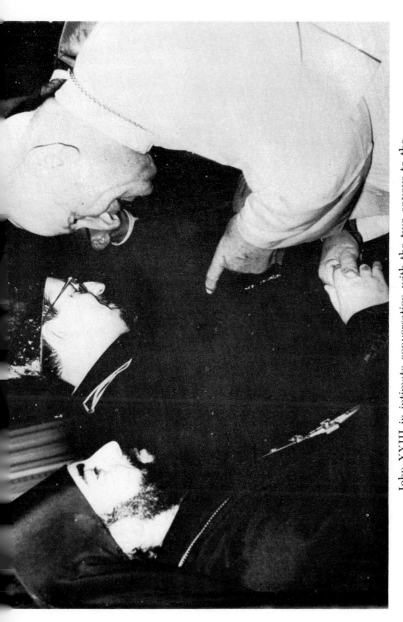

John XXIII in intimate conversation with the two envoys to the Council from the Russian Orthodox Church, Vladimir Kotlyarov and Vitaly Borovoi.

Panorama of the Council in session in the nave of St. Peter's
Basilica, looking toward the high altar where
the Pope's throne is located.

Pope John addressing the Council Fathers in the final meeting
of the first session of Vatican II, December 8, 1962.

John XXIII and the Cardinal Archbishop of Milan,
Giovanni Battista Montini, the future Pope Paul VI.

"You are a consolation to the Church."
These are the last words I heard
from Good Pope John.

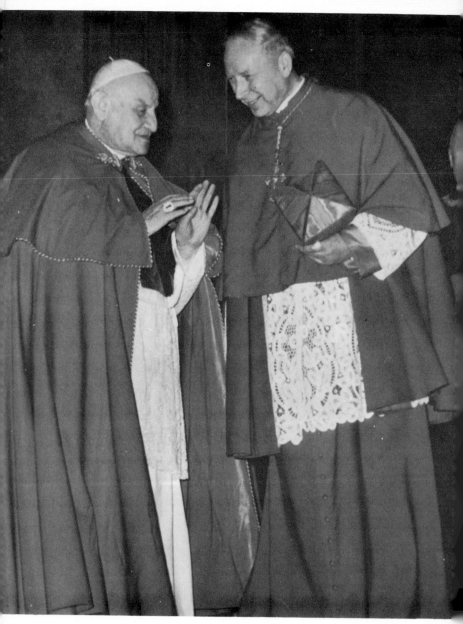

The Pope's concern for the "Church of Silence" manifested itself
in many ways. Here he is conferring with the Primate of Poland,
Stefan Cardinal Wyszynski.

As the Bishop of Rome, Pope John kept the needs of his flock close to his heart. During the Lenten Season, he visited many of the churches in and about the city. When he spoke to his faithful, *Papa Giovanni* never failed to express his joy at finding himself in their midst and his desire to bring to each one of them a word of comfort and peace.

Returning to the Vatican from a parish in Ostia, Pope John had his driver stop briefly alongside the streamlined Fumicino airport where he could watch the jet arrivals and departures.

On May 10, 1963, the "Pope of Peace" was presented with the Balzan Peace Prize for 1963 in the Sala Regia of the Vatican. Pope John's brief discourse on this occasion ended with the following lines: "Peace is a house—the house of all men. It is the arch that joins earth to heaven. But to rise so high it must rest on four pillars: truth, justice, charity and freedom."

Pope John's final trip outside the
Vatican was his historic visit to the
Quirinal on May 11, 1963. Above
the Pope greets Antonio Segni,
President of Italy,
outside the Quirinal.

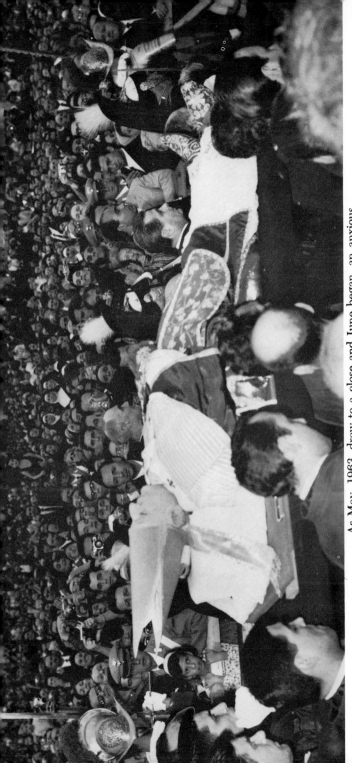

As May, 1963, drew to a close and June began, an anxious world watched and prayed. *Papa Giovanni* was seriously ill and death was drawing slowly near.

After a four-day agony, Good Pope John went to meet his Master—June 3, 1963. His body was borne in solemn procession through St. Peter's Square, while a tearful throng looked for a last time on the Pope of Goodness.

Pope John's body lying in state in St. Peter's Basilica.

The simple tomb of John XXIII near that of Pope Pius XI.
At some future date his body will be entombed in the Basilica
of St. John Lateran, according to his express wish.

SEGRETERIA DI STATO

N. 104.797

Dal Vaticano, li **June 12, 1963**

Your Eminence,

I have the honor to forward to Your Eminence the enclosed pectoral cross which was destined by the Holy Father John XXIII for Your Eminence.

This cross was used by His Holiness during the years of His service for the Holy See in the Orient, in Paris and Venice. It was also used by Him while He was Pope.

I gladly take this occasion to renew to Your Eminence the sentiments of my deep respect and cordial regard.

Devotedly yours in Christ,

+ A. gee Argen
Archbishop

His Eminence
Richard Cardinal Cushing
Archbishop of Boston
North American College
ROME

(Enclosure - pectoral cross)

makes to the economic effort, the financial state of the company for which he works, the requirements of the general good of the particular country—having regard especially for the repercussions on the overall employment of the working force in the country as a whole—and finally the requirements of the common good of the universal family of nations of every kind, both large and small.

"The above principles are valid always and everywhere! So much is clear. But their degree of applicability to concrete cases cannot be determined without reference to the quantity and quality of available resources; and these can—and in fact do—vary from country to country, and even, from time to time, within the same country."

INTER-RACIAL HARMONY

"If communities of varying racial backgrounds are to succeed in living together peacefully as people so eagerly desire, the first thing needed is for all animosity to be put aside and 'thoughts of peace and not affliction' to be nourished. May the bright star of a lasting harmony between brothers . . . begin to shine; and may the peoples that are reaching out to achieve the goal of a peaceful and productive life together find an answer and fulfillment for their legitimate desires.

"It causes the Pastor of the universal flock of Christ intense pain to see the conditions of suffering, hardship and insecurity in which so many of his sons find themselves. How could he help feeling sad deep within him at the thought of the difficulties they are going through, since his paternal interest and care reach out to all of them without exception?

"May the Redeeming Blood of the Savior of all peoples make all men no longer strangers, nor enemies, but brothers; may it strengthen their determination to achieve peace, their hopes and desires for tranquility and prosperity; may it smother every germ of division and of rivalry, so that mutual love, the basis for lasting Christian civilization, may spread and hold sway."

THE BOND OF MATRIMONY

"In the face of the uncertainties and doubts of a doctrinal nature that can be found here and there in various forms and that are threatening to mislead public opinion, we need a solemn and serious reminder of the solid principles that inspire the Church in its defense of matrimony. In safeguarding the indissolubility of the bond and the holiness of the Great Sacrament with jealous care, the Church is defending something that is not just ecclesiastical and civil law, but principally natural and divine positive law. These two great and necessary goods, that are sometimes hidden behind the veil of passions and prejudices to the point where they are forgotten entirely, are based on something prior to positive law–on the natural law engraved in indelible letters on the human conscience in the one case, and on the divine law of Our Lord Jesus Christ in the other.

"And so it is not a question of rules and regulations that are imposed because of circumstances and that can change in the course of time: instead it is a case of the divine will, of the untouchable order established by God Himself to safeguard the basic unit of civil society. It is a question of the original divine law that has, in the fullness of time, been brought back to its genuine integrity by the words of Christ 'From the beginning it was not so' (Matt. 19:8)."

DISARMAMENT

"Justice, right reason and consideration for human dignity and life urgently demand that the arms race should cease; that the stockpiles which exist in various countries should be reduced equally and simultaneously by the parties concerned; that nuclear weapons should be banned; and finally that all come to an agreement on a fitting program of disarmament, employing mutual and effective controls. In the words of Pius XII, Our Predecessor of happy memory: 'The calamity of a world war, with the economic and social ruin and the moral excesses and dissolution that accompany it, must not be permitted to envelop the human race for a third time.'

"All must realize that there is no hope of putting an end to the building up of armaments, nor of reducing the present stocks, nor, still less—and this is the main point—of abolishing them altogether, unless the process is complete and thorough and unless it proceeds from inner conviction: unless, that is, everyone sincerely cooperates to banish the fear and anxious expectation of war with which men are oppressed. If this is to come about, the fundamental principle on which our present peace depends must be replaced by another, which declares that the true and solid peace of nations consists not in equality of arms but in mutual trust alone. We believe that this can be brought to pass, and we consider that, since it concerns a matter not only demanded by right reason but also eminently desirable in itself, it will prove to be the source of many benefits."

SCIENTIFIC PROGRESS AND TRUE VALUES

"It has been claimed that in an era of scientific and technical triumph such as ours man can well afford to rely on his powers, and construct a very good civilization without God. But the truth is that these very advances in science and technology frequently involve the whole human race in such difficulties as can only be solved in the light of a sincere faith in God, the Creator and Ruler of man and his world.

"The almost limitless horizons opened up by scientific research only go to confirm this truth. More and more men are beginning to realize that science has so far done little more than scratch the surface of nature and reality. There are vast hidden depths still to be explored and adequately explained. Such men are appalled when they consider how these gigantic forces for good can be turned by science into engines of destruction. They realize then the importance of spiritual and moral values, if scientific and technical progress are to be used in the service of civilization, and not involve the whole human race in irremediable disaster.

"Furthermore, the increasing sense of dissatisfaction with worldly goods which is making itself felt among citizens of the wealthier nations, is rapidly destroying the treasured illusion of an earthly paradise. Men, too, are becoming more and more conscious of their rights as human beings, rights which are universal and inviolable; and they are aspiring to more just and more human relations with their fellows. The effect of all this is to make the modern man more deeply aware of his own limitations, and to create in him a striving for spiritual values, all of which encourages us in the hope that individuals and nations will one day unite in a spirit of sincere understanding and profitable cooperation."

TRIBUTES TO POPE JOHN

FROM WORLD LEADERS

AND MEN OF ALL FAITHS

Pope John XXIII was a pastoral Pope. The Ecumenical Council he called was a pastoral Council, not necessarily a doctrinal Council. The Council, itself, I am confident, will make a great contribution in promoting brotherhood among all people and unity among all Christians. However, the personal qualities of John XXIII, namely, his kindness, benevolence, charity, love for all men, his vision and his courage were among the greatest contributions for promoting brotherhood.

Pope John played a very important role in world affairs by his personal contacts with religious leaders of all faiths and with political leaders who called to see him. He was opposed to all forms of tyranny and dictatorship, but he was dedicated to the dignity of the individual person and loved all people. It is reported, for example, that he said to the son-in-law of Khruschev when he and his wife visited the Vatican, "You say you are an atheist but won't you permit an old man to give a blessing to your children?"

Personal contacts of that kind gave Pope John a very important role in world affairs because they were personal and without any ulterior motive, save the good of humanity. Thus the whole human family was desolate when it learned of the death of this universal Father. Eulogies and tributes from men of all ranks and faiths were unanimous in their esteem and love for the "Pope of Goodness".

*   *   *

"The highest work of any man is to protect and carry on the deepest spiritual heritage of the race. To Pope John was given the almost unique gift of enriching and enlarging that tradition.

"Armed with the humility and calm which surrounded his earliest days, he brought compassion and an understanding drawn from wide experience to the most divisive problems of a tumultuous age. He was the chosen leader of world Catholicism; but his concern for the human spirit transcended all boundaries of belief or geography.

"The enabling precepts of his encyclicals and his actions drew on the accumulated wisdom of an ancient faith for guidance in the most complex and troublesome problems of the modern age.

"To him the divine spark that unites men would ultimately prove more enduring than the forces which divide. His wisdom, compassion and kindly strength has bequeathed humanity a new legacy of purpose and courage for the future."

The Late President John F. Kennedy

"We shall always remember Pope John's great pastoral qualities and his leadership in the Ecumenical movement."

President Lyndon B. Johnson

"A most noble life has come to an end, and its epitome of the highest human qualities is no longer with us. The death of His Holiness Pope John XXIII was deeply felt by men everywhere who saw in him a symbol of universality, peace and harmony.

"Although he was the head of the Roman Catholic Church, Pope John XXIII in his memorable encyclical, *Pacem in Terris,* spoke for all men and to all men in restating his belief in the dignity of the individual, in fundamental human rights, in justice, and in an effective international order.

"His was truly an ecumenical message of far-sighted significance. History offers few examples where the affection and respect of mankind have been so overwhelmingly centered on one single human being as in the case of His Holiness, John XXIII. That this respect and affection should have developed in such a short period of time and should have transcended both national and religious boundaries is even more rare.

"In identifying himself so unreservedly with the cause of peace and international understanding, Pope John XXIII became the very embodiment of mankind's own aspirations in this uncertain period of history. It is therefore fitting that the Pope's last moments on this earth should have been accompanied by what the Vatican has aptly called a plebiscite of prayer.

"The thinking and actions of Pope John XXIII were unfailingly guided by a full measure of confidence in the potentialities of mankind. Let this confidence be a source of inspiration to us all, so that we, too, may usefully serve the cause of peace and understanding among men."

U THANT, Secretary-General, UN General Assembly

"His Holiness will be universally mourned, not only as a great prince of the Roman Catholic Church, but also as a great humanitarian."

Zafrulla Khan, President UN General Assembly

"We retain good memories of John XXIII, whose fruitful activities for the maintenance and strengthening of peace earned him wide recognition and won him the respect of peace-loving peoples."

Nikita Khruschev

"On this sad occasion Her Majesty and the Duke of Edinburgh recall the impressive memories of their meeting with His Holiness in 1961. Her Majesty has greatly appreciated the kindly feelings which His Holiness has always exhibited toward herself and her subjects."

Queen Elizabeth II

"The Pope was a person to whom all men might look with profound respect . . ."

Keith Holyoake, Prime Minister of New Zealand

"The Holy Father's wisdom and charity endeared him to all our hearts."

Eamon De Valera, President of Ireland

"His sanctity, charity and magnanimity will long remain a source of inspiration to the whole world."

Sean Lemass, Premier of Ireland

"The death of the Sovereign Pontiff, all of whose reign has been consecrated to peace among men and to a rapprochment among Christians, is felt with grief by the people of France."

Charles De Gaulle

"Pope John has taken his place in history among the great popes in his fight for peace."

Heinrich Luebke, President of West Germany

The Pope was "a man of great heart and an eminent spokesman for peaceful co-existence and understanding among nations."

Aleksander Zawadski, President of Poland

"Pope John dedicated his life to solving the great problems of our epoch."

Janos Kadar, Premier of Hungary

"In this hour of mourning, the Pope's great teachings shine more than ever and the memory of the work he did for the good of the Church and for the whole of humanity within the short span of a few years is re-enkindled."

Antonio Segni, President of Italy

"Pope John worked with untiring labor toward bringing Christians closer together and strengthening the desire for peace among men."

Konrad Adenauer

"Pope John's teachings will remain as a sure inspiration for the good government of peoples."

General Francisco Franco

"All humanity mourns the death of a great Pope of peace."

Joao Goulart, President of Brazil

"Pope John XXIII . . . contributed greatly to the new brotherly relationships of the churches believing in the one Lord."

The World Council of Churches

"In every part of Christendom there is grief at the passing of a great Christian leader."

Michael Ramsey, Archbishop of Canterbury

"The reign of Pope John XXIII was marked by fruitful activity for the sake of consolidating peace and peaceful cooperation among nations."

Tass, the official Soviet news agency

"The life of the great Pontiff was sanctified and devoted to the development of mutual comprehension between all peoples of the world and to overall peace."

Shneor Zalman Shazar, President of Israel

The Pope's death was "a loss not only to the Catholic Church but to the whole of humanity."

Adolph Schaerf, President of Austria

". . . not only Catholics but all people everywhere take leave of this simple man with great sorrow."

Radio Warsaw

Jews have suffered "the loss of one of the greatest humanitarians of our century."

Dr. Zrah Wahrhaftig, Religious Affairs Minister, Israel

Pope John was for the Philippines "its spiritual leader, fatherly guide and friend."

Diosdado Macapagal, President of the Philippines

"Before his reign Christians of different creeds regarded each other with respect but not with any special affection. Pope John altered all that."

John C. Heenan, Archbishop of
Liverpool, England

"Pope John's friendly attitude to the powers from the East arose from his belief that it was his mission to

demonstrate the openness and goodness of his Lord. . . .
It was not in his character to fight against something. He
preferred to fight for something."

Bernard Cardinal Alfrink, Archbishop of Utrecht

"The Pope used his office and his energy to bring
peace and to oppose policies which lead to war and mass
murder."

Bertrand Russell

Pope John's "great thoughts. . . bold plans. . . simplicity and warmth. . . won him honor and love far beyond the borders of his Church."

Otto Dibelius, Evangelical Bishop of Berlin

"John XXIII wished his pontificate to be pastoral
in nature. The words of his coronation homily left no
doubt about this intention, and every action of his pontificate seems to confirm the pastoral imprint, whether in
his spoken word or in the decisions made by him.

"Indeed I would say that the pastoral pontificate of
Pope John took on gigantic dimensions in the short space
of the less than five years accorded to him by Christ to
rule over His Church.

"Pope John truly exemplified the words of the Divine Master as they are recorded in the Acts of the
Apostles by St. Luke, when he says of Jesus 'Jesus did
and taught.'

"From the very beginning of his pontificate, Pope
John began by doing things in a big way, first in his own
life through the abundant manifestations of charity which

captured the imagination and the attention of the world, and then in the practical application to the pastoral problems which faced the Church."

Albert Gregory Cardinal Meyer
Archbishop of Chicago

"Pope John seems to have been sent particularly for this era, this time, this circumstance in the world, and it is quite unique to notice that the people of the world have sensed in his attitude toward the unity of all people —out of love and devotion, because we are the creatures of God and therefore created all equally, and destined for a unity with God—that has been the prime motive of his writings, of his utterances, and of his prayers."

James Francis Cardinal McIntyre
Archbishop of Los Angeles

"Even in our sorrow, we are grateful to God for giving us Pope John XXIII. He was a Pope for our times. I recall with emotion the eloquent sermon he delivered on the morning of his coronation in St. Peter's. He quoted from the Gospel of St. John.

" 'Other sheep I have that are not of this fold. Them also I must bring, and they shall hear my voice, and there shall be one fold and one shepherd.'

"This was the vision that fired his priestly heart. He lived and died consumed by it. May all men of all faiths whom our Holy Father loved so ardently, and for whom he labored so tirelessly, beseech Almighty God to grant eternal rest and happiness to his Vicar, Pope John XXIII."

Francis Cardinal Spellman, Archbishop of New York

" 'This Pope will do great good for the Church, even more by his goodness than by his knowledge.' These words were written to me by a high Vatican official not more than a month after the election of John XXIII. Those who encountered Pope John personally were struck most by the gentleness and humility that always marked his dealings with others and his references to himself. His exalted position never diminished his sense of humor. We have lost not only a great spiritual leader for the Church, but a spiritual father and a close friend."

Most Rev. Charles P. Greco, Bishop of Alexandria, La.

"John XXIII broke many of the precedents, such as increasing the traditional number in the College of Cardinals, and including members for the first time from Africa, Japan, and the Philippine Islands.

"From the point of view of the intellectual impact of his work, the preparation for the Council has stirred up interest both directly and indirectly in many important fields. This interest has not been restricted to the specialist, but has reached down to the man in the street. Consequently, we find that the great theological issues are now being discussed widely by non-Catholics as well as Catholics, by the laity as well as the clergy. So, too, are questions of liturgy, of Christian education, and many others. Undoubtedly, enthusiasm for the exploration of such topics will continue.

"Of Pope John's eight encyclicals, the two best known are *Mater et Magistra* and *Pacem in Terris*. The former deals mainly with economic problems in the light of Christian principles, and while it adds little to the doctrine of Pope Leo XIII, and Pope Pius XI, it did make a distinctive contribution by showing that Pope John was considerably alert to the needs of the contemporary world, as well as to the spirit of our time.

"His other great encyclical, that on peace, was addressed to all men of good will, and received universal acclaim. It called for disarmament, elimination of racism, and the voluntary establishment of a world authority capable of upholding the common good of the world community. While making clear that communism is intrinsically wrong, it indicated that it may be possible to work with communist states or movements in the interest of good causes. These encyclicals provide material for study and application for future generations.

"Of enduring significance, also, was the stress laid by Pope John on the great related concepts of charity, unity and peace. Because of the personal exemplification of these cherished objectives, his life was an inspiration and his memory will be a benediction."

Rt. Rev. Msgr. William J. McDonald
Rector of Catholic University of America

"I will never forget the opening service at St. Peter's last autumn, when in a beautiful allocution addressed to the 2,500 bishops who were present from all over the world, Pope John injected a remark—the observers, you see, there were 40 of us from Protestantism, from Anglicanism, from Eastern Orthodoxy, and other groups—he said, 'It comforts me greatly to know that my brethren, the observers, are present with us.' Now you must realize that in Latin, the word 'comfort' means not just console. It also means strengthen, and encourage.

"Now Pope John said that it was an encouragement to him, strengthened his hand, so to speak, lifted
up his heart a little bit, to know that the observers were
there and that they were sympathetic and listening with
great sympathy, and sharing in the service too–because
we did; every morning we were there at the Mass.

"All this touched us very deeply, and I must say
that when later in the session one of the bishops–(the
bishops were limited to ten minutes; the speeches were
all in Latin, and they were brief, and they usually began
"Reverendissimi Patris," etc., in Latin–"Most Reverend
Fathers" addressing the bishops and the cardinals)–one
of them added a day or two later 'and beloved brethren
of the observers.'

"Well, when in the world could that ever have happened before, I mean in the past four or five hundred
years, and how could it ever have happened without the
dominant spirit of that one great Christian, Pope John?"

Dr. Frederick Grant, Episcopalian observer
at the Ecumenical Council representing
the Anglican Communion

"I would doubt whether any previous Pope has so
won the affection and respect of Protestants as John
XXIII. He has commended both himself and his office
as none of his predecessors, and it may well be that the
Council which was largely his work may represent a real
turning point in the history of Christianity.

"To be sure, there were many currents of thought
before him, but he has given them an influence and a
power they would scarcely have achieved otherwise. He

has helped to mitigate what was the great scandal of all Christianity, that those who sought to testify to the power of God's reconciliation showed so little of it among themselves.

"His hope was not so much for institutional reunion of the churches as it was for their inner renewal, both of the Roman Catholic Church, and of other Christian bodies. And sure in this he was right.

"Only as all of the churches grow up into and understand the power of the new life in Christ, Jesus, will there be any hope of institutional reunion. And before that day, there will be many things they can do to strengthen each other's hand.

"I am sure that I would be expressing the feelings of millions of Protestants when I express gratitude for this warm and devoted pastor, and the hope that he may have a successor who will continue the work of the Council."

Dr. James H. Nichols, Princeton Theological Seminary

"I think there is no question but that Pope John has instituted a religious movement which is the most significant movement in world history in this present century. It is very evident from all of his statements, as well as his own attitudes as an example, that he was sincerely interested in making the fellowship between all Christians a happier and a better fellowship.

"Therefore, he has already said, as you know, that we must recapture the working man, and that is the common undertaking of all Christians, and that brotherhood must precede doctrine. And I am very sure that what Pope John, because of his unusual personality—it was my great privilege to have an hour's private audience with Pope John and to see him at close range under many conditions—that with his wonderful spirit and attitude, and his fine understanding of the true meaning of Christian fellowship, that this movement that he has begun will continue, and that the relationships between Christians will be more united to fight our common enemies, and try to make this world a really Christian world."

Bishop Fred P. Corson, World Methodist Council

"It may be safely predicted that when the annals of the 20th century are definitively recorded many decades hence, the name of Angelo Giuseppe Roncalli will appear as one of the half dozen most creative and influential figures of that century.

"It is probable that it will be because of his influence upon the spiritual climate of the world, and especially of the relations of Roman Catholics to other Christians that Pope John's pre-eminence will be recognized.

"A year ago at this time neither the most far-sighted nor optimistic prophet would have dared to forecast the transformation of climate and the alteration in relationships which the past months have witnessed, and these have been due, more than to all other factors together, to the vision, initiative and indomitable determination of this one man. But behind these achievements which all mankind recognize and praise lie two qualities of the person himself which are the true secrets of his greatness.

"On the one hand, his sensitivity and responsiveness to the direction of God's spirit. It has been too little stressed that the very idea of the Vatican Council, through which these great historic accomplishments have been effected, came to the Pope in a private revelation analogous to the inspirations which have guided and ruled the greatest spiritual seers of all time, the kind of immediate disclosure of divine purpose which is so largely absent from and disdained—if not distrusted—by the sophisticated mind of our secularized age.

"Second, the qualities of humaneness; earthy common sense and all-embracing compassion which have endeared Pope John to millions beyond, as well as within his own Church, and for which he is beloved and revered by the simple as well as the wise of his fellow men."

Dr. Henry P. Van Dusen
Retired President, Union Theological Seminary

"Pope John gave currency to the phrase 'separated brethren,' to describe those of us who are outside the visible structure of the Roman Catholic Church, and for him the noun was basic rather than the adjective.

"To him, we were first of all brethren, and only secondarily and tragically separated.

"That so much has happened in so little time to improve the climate of understanding between Catholics and Protestants is something that we must attribute to the initiative and leadership of Pope John, though to be totally accurate, we would have to assign the reason for this, as he would have done, not to himself, but to the Holy Spirit.

"He beckoned the Catholic Church to move out toward the separated brethren as far as she could in fidelity to her own convictions, and to engage in that renewal which is always the Church's task, and the task upon which Christendom is always most loathe to embark.

"It must therefore be our prayer that the concerns of Pope John, too manifest throughout the first session of Vatican Council II, will be brought to fruition when the Council reconvenes under the order of Pope John's successor.

"He has led the way, and the completion by his fellow bishops of that which he initiated will be the most signal mark of honor his own Church can bestow upon him.

" 'Survey the history of the Papal See over the past several centuries,' the Protestant theologian Karl Barth once remarked. 'I cannot hear the voice of the Good Shepherd in this See of Peter.' Those of us among the separated brethren—Karl Barth now included—find that comment a very dated one since the Pontificate of John XXIII. In him we have heard the voice of the Good Shepherd, solicitous for those outside as well as within the sheepfold.

"Catholics have lost a Pope; we have lost a friend and brother."

Professor Robert McAfee Brown
Professor of Religion
Stanford University

"John XXIII will be recorded through history as the first Roman Catholic Pontiff after the 11th Century who understood today's needs and tried to do something about them.

"His passing finds him in the middle of an historical point of his Church. The Greek Archdiocese of North and South America, and Archbishop Iakovos personally, will mourn for long the loss of this real humanitarian and ecclesiastical leader who might have been one of the main instruments for the Ecumenical movement also."

Chancellor Germanos, Greek Orthodox Church

"An Archbishop of Canterbury hadn't spoken personally to a Pope for over 400 years. You might think it was a bit embarrassing when the Archbishop of Canterbury for the first time thus talked to a Pope. There was no embarrassment of any kind whatsoever on either side, and that for a very good reason: that we greeted each other as straightforward, earnest, humble Christian brethren. And when I have said that, I have said all there is to it.

"We started off—there was never a dull moment in the whole hour—it was full of liveliness. We talked about our own spiritual experiences, and that is what friends naturally do.

"Now that was my vivid experience of an hour with him, but it wasn't the first knowledge I had of his personality. Many years ago, he was the Papal representative in Istanbul, and there in Istanbul, we had our Chaplain, and the one who was later to be Pope used to drop in to tea with him frequently, and our bishop there was a Bishop of Gibralter, and he and the future Pope used to go out for walks together.

"Now you can see at once what kind of a person the Pope was. Wherever he was, he wanted to be friends with Christian friends, and that is what he brought to his Papacy. That is what he has given to the whole Church. And what has happened as a result of his reign is that all over the world, churchmen of different churches are now able to talk together as friends, to discuss their differences as friends and not as enemies, not arguing and controverting one another, but trying to understand one another and walk together in the Lord, or in the spirit.

"Now that is a complete revolution. It is incredible that such a change should have taken place within four or five years. It is here in England; it is in all parts of the world. What happens is that somebody says to me, 'Do you know, for first time in my life, the Roman priests have come to call on me'; or 'for the first time in our lives, we have had a little meeting of the ministers of all the churches, including the Roman Catholic Church, and the Roman priest has said a prayer along with us.'

"All those are terribly simple things, but they belong to the Kingdom of God, which our Lord preached."

Dr. Geoffrey Fisher, Former Archbishop of Canterbury

"Religious life in America has benefited enormously because of the bold, liberalizing ministry of Pope John. Because of him, leaders of the three faiths are involved in an exchange of thought and activity, heretofore considered impossible. Before Pope John, many people thought that the Church was a monolith, one voice, one view, frozen in history like Lot's wife, immobile, ever looking backward theologically.

"Now we know that there are varying opinions in the Church, and we hear them, and we see many colors, and tones, and hues, and we know the Church is not monochromatic, nor is it frozen into rigidity, but flexible and capable of adjustment.

"Some religious leaders labor together today more effectively and frequently, as the Conference on Race and Religion in Chicago demonstrated. There are today innumerable monologues, dialogues, triologues, and no longer do they simply whistle to the deaf, as one observer had it.

"A group of Protestant clergymen invited a New England Cardinal to visit with them, and he had them, in turn, with a group of his priests at a retreat. A West Coast bishop inquired whether Rabbis would work with him and his staff on problems of mutual concern.

"There is a thaw in many parts of American religious life because of the warm liberality of Pope John, and a portent for a better religious climate.

"Pope John lived long enough for glory, but an insufficient time for mankind."

Rabbi Jacob Kaufman, United Hebrew Congregations

"All my contacts with Pope John made me sense his true greatness as a creative Christian leader. He was a spiritual pioneer, who, in asking for renewal of the Church, opened up new prospects for a united Christendom."

Doctor Stanley Stuber, Executive Secretary
Missouri Council of Churches

"Christians of all Churches extend sympathy to their Roman Catholic brethren in the loss of their spiritual leader and join with them in thanksgiving to Almighty God for the dedicated Christian life and witness of Pope John XXIII.

"The Pope's tireless efforts for world peace and Christian unity have already effected widespread improvement in the climate of human relationships and have inspired countless people to new endeavors for the spiritual and material welfare of all mankind. The courage and winsomeness of his example will have enduring influence and will continue to bear fruit both within and beyond the Roman Catholic Church."

Doctor Roswell P. Barnes
World Council of Churches

"Very many important developments have taken place during Pope John's pontificate. But most important of all, has been that profound change in relationships that has led to the beginning of a true dialogue between the Roman Catholic Church and other Churches. I believe that Pope John XXIII will be remembered as the Pope who made that new dialogue possible."

Dr. W. A. Visser't Hooft, Secretary General
WCC, Geneva, Switzerland

"The death of Pope John is the end of a saintly Christian life and the promise of a new period leading to new relations among Christians and the brotherhood of man.

"All faiths will sorely miss Pope John. Christianity will mourn him but the Christians of the world can never think of him in terms of a great loss, for he has been the great gain in the cause for Christian unity and peace."

Archbishop Iakovos, Greek Orthodox Archdiocese
of North and South America

"The Pope's death will be mourned by multitudes of people around the world who felt the impact of his personal sincerity and goodness.

"Baptists join in paying tribute to his memory, not as the powerful Pontifex of the Roman Catholic Church but as a fellow Christian who sought to be a bridge-builder beween all those who profess devotion to Jesus Christ."

Dr. Josef Nordenhaug, Baptist World Alliance, Washington, D.C.

"The hearts of Christians of every confession are united to a degree that is unique for many centuries at the death of the universally esteemed and beloved John XXIII, the Pope of Unity.

"Thanks to God who gave him to our generation. All of us would have wished for him to live on, throwing open doors of understanding and thawing the antagonisms that have separated Christian brethren. Our prayer is that the warmth of his spirit will not be chilled and the height of his vision will not shrink."

Dr. Franklin Fry, Lutheran World Federation

"Protestant and Eastern Orthodox Christians join with their Roman Catholic brothers in this time of great loss. We are consoled only in knowing that Pope John gave so much in the short span of his holy office, and that he has left as his heritage a reawakened spirit of unity of love that will be felt forever by men of faith."

Dr. Roy G. Ross, National Council of Churches

"Pope John was a foremost spiritual leader, not only in the vast areas of the Church of Rome, but among countless thousands throughout the world.

"The new direction given to inter-religious understanding by Pope John XXIII will continue as a living memorial to his life of dedication to the service of his Lord."

Dr. Arthur Lee Kinsolving
Protestant Council of the City of New York

"The whole world suffers a deep loss at the Pope's death. Despite the shortness of his reign which represents not an interlude but an epoch he will go down in history as making one of the most significant contributions in modern times to peace and goodwill among men.

"The Pope was an intuitive judge of mankind's hopes and needs ... who pushed the Catholic Church squarely into the Twentieth Century by setting the stage for far-reaching adjustments designed to cope with revolutionary, scientific, political, social and economic changes sweeping the modern world."

Dr. Lewis Webster Jones
National Conference of Christians and Jews

"Members of the Jewish faith join our brethren of the Roman Catholic Church in expressing our profound grief on the passing of Pope John XXIII.

"Through his simplicity, his modesty and his dedication to the establishment of brotherhood, justice and peace in the world, he brought hope to untold millions of men and women of all faiths, races and nations."

Dr. Julius Mark
Senior Rabbi, Temple Emmanuel, New York City

"His Holiness, Pope John XXIII, was a personality of prophetic stature. His was a voice, benevolent and strong in behalf of peace, based upon spiritual principles. I sincerely hope that his voice in death will be heard as it was in his lifetime. I extend sincere condolences to my brethren, the communicants of the Catholic Church."

Doctor Albert G. Minda
President, Central Conference of American Rabbis

"The pontiff's extraordinary personal leadership that has significantly transformed and improved human relationships in such an historic way . . . may well constitute his greatest living monument.

"Jewish history will regard Pope John as 'one of the righteous among the nations of the earth who earned a place in the world to come.' The Pope's spirit will continue to radiate in the relationships between man and his fellows for years to come."

A. M. Sonnabend
President, American Jewish Committee

"Everywhere Christians will grieve in the death of Pope John. We thank God for his life and ministry. He has given to his own Church a new openness to other

Christians as all of us seek to proclaim the Gospel of Christ to a seeking world."

Doctor Fredrik Schiotz
President, American Lutheran Church

"The death of Pope John is a great loss not only to his fellow Catholics, who looked to him as their Holy Father, but also to Protestants and Jews. Pope John saw all human beings as children of God."

Rabbi Roland G. Gittelsohn
President of the Jewish Community Council of
Metropolitan Boston

"Few men have influenced the world as Pope John XXIII. His leadership has been primarily a leadership of the heart.

"The Roman Catholic Church touches men of every nation and influences their lives. In the Pope this largest segment of Christendom has had a leader who has led his church into paths of deeper devotion and in ways of greater helpfulness to all mankind. The Vatican Council has already profoundly affected its life for all time."

Rt. Rev. Anson Stokes Jr., representing the
Protestant Episcopal Dioceses of Massachusetts

"The death of Pope John XXIII is a great loss not only for the Catholic Church but for mankind. He was an exceptional man who had the profound perception of the human situation and the common problems and aspirations of people of our day."

Father John Zanetos
Dean of the Greek Cathedral, Boston

"During the serious illness of Pope John XXIII, multitudes of Protestants were concerned and prayed for him. Protestants stand as one with their Roman Catholic brethren in experiencing a deep sense of loss."

Methodist Bishop James K. Mathews, President,
Massachusetts Council of Churches

"The passing of Pope John is a severe loss to all of civilized mankind. His broad compassion and profound concern for people and their welfare was truly universal. His love encompassed men of all faiths, all nations and all races. In his person he sympathized and epitomized the common touch and the divine spark. May his memory be a blessing. His life surely was."

Rabbi Murray I. Rothman

THE LAST WILL AND TESTAMENT

OF JOHN XXIII

VENICE

June 29, 1954

On the point of presenting myself to the Lord, One and Triune, Who created me and redeemed me and wished to have me as His priest and Bishop, Who showered me with unending blessings, I entrust my soul to His mercy; I humbly beg His pardon for my sins and for my shortcomings.

I offer to Him the little good that with His help I have succeeded in doing, though imperfect and poor, for His glory, for the service of the Holy Church, for the edification of my brothers, begging Him finally to receive me, as a good and pious Father, among His saints into a blessed eternity.

I wish to profess wholly once again my Christian and Catholic Faith, my adherence and subservience to the Holy, Apostolic and Roman Church, and my perfect devotion and obedience to its august head, the Supreme Pontiff, whom it was my great honor to represent for many years in different regions of the East and West, and who wished to have me in Venice as Cardinal and Patriarch, and whom I have always followed with sincere affection, apart from every dignity conferred upon me.

The sense of my littleness and nothingness has always kept me good company, keeping me humble and quiet and affording me the joy of devoting myself as best I could to the constant practice of obedience and charity for souls and to the interests of the Kingdom of Jesus, my Lord and my All. To Him be all glory; may my only reward be His mercy. You are my All, my Lord. You know that I love You. For me this is enough.

I ask the forgiveness of those whom I have offended unconsciously and of those to whom I may not have given good example. I feel that I have nothing to forgive anyone, for I recognize as brothers and benefactors all those who knew me or had any dealings with me–even should they have offended me, scorned me, not held me in esteem, or may have caused me sorrow, as they have done rightly.

Born poor, but of honorable and humble people, I am particularly happy to die poor, having distributed all that came into my hands during the years of my priesthood and my episcopate–which in fact has been rather limited–according to the needs and circumstances of my simple and modest life, for the service to the poor and to Holy Church which nurtured me. Appearances of comfortable circumstances often concealed hidden thorns of afflicting poverty and prevented me from always giving with the generosity which I desired.

I thank God for this grace of poverty which I vowed in my youth, poverty of spirit as a priest of the Sacred Heart and real poverty which sustained me in never asking for anything, neither positions, money nor favors; never, neither for myself nor for my relatives or my friends.

To my beloved family of the flesh, from whom I did not in fact receive any material wealth, I can leave only a very great and a very special blessing, with the exhortation that it preserve that fear of God which made it so dear and beloved to me. That family, though simple and modest without shame, is my only real title of nobility.

I have always helped it in its most urgent needs, as a poor man of the poor, but without taking it out of its honorable and contented poverty. I pray and will always pray that it may prosper, happy as I am to see in new and vigorous offspring the steadfastness and faithfulness to the religious traditions of our fathers which will always be its real wealth. My most fervent wish is that no member of my family and relatives may ever miss the joy of the final eternal meeting.

Queste pagine scritte da me valgono come attestazione della mia volontà assoluta per + caso di una mia morte 29 giugno 1954 improvvisa. + Ang. Gius. card. Roncalli

Venezia.

Testamento Spirituale e mie ultime volontà.

E valgono come Testamento Venezia 17 ? ottobre 1957

da aggiungersi alle disposizioni +

in quella

Sul punto di ripresentarmi al Signore Uno e Trino, che mi creò, mi redense, mi volle suo sacerdote e vescovo, mi colmo di grazie senza fine, affido la povera anima mia alla sua misericordia: gli chiedo umilmente perdono dei miei peccati e delle mie deficienze: gli offro quel po' di bene che col suo aiuto mi è riuscito di fare anche se imperfetto e meschino, a gloria sua, a servizio della S.Chiesa, ad edificazione dei miei fratelli, supplicandolo infine di accogliermi, come padre buono e pio, coi santi suoi nella beata eternità.

Amo di professare ancora una volta tutta intera la mia fede cristiana e cattolica, e la mia appartenenza e soggezione alla Santa Chiesa Apostolica e Romana, e la mia perfetta devozione ed obbedienza al suo Capo Augusto il Sommo Pontefice, che fu mio grande onore di rappresentare per lunghi anni nelle varie regioni di Oriente e di Occidente, che mi volle infine a Venezia come Cardinale e Patriarca, e che ho sempre seguito con affezione sincera, al di fuori e al di sopra di ogni dignità conferitami. Il senso della mia pochezza e del mio niente mi ha sempre fatto buona compagnia tenendomi umile e quieto, e concedendomi la gioia di impiegarmi del mio meglio in esercizio continuato di obbedienza e di carità per le anime e per gli interessi del Regno di Gesù, mio Signore e mio tutto. A lui tutta la gloria: per me ed a merito mio la sua misericordia. Meritum meum miseratio Domini. Domine, tu omnia nosti: tu scis quia amo Te. Questo solo mi basta. - Chiedo perdono a coloro che avessi inconsciamente offeso: a quanti non avessi recato edificazione. Sento di non aver nulla da perdonare a nichessia, perchè in quanti mi conobbero ed ebbero rapporti con me - mi avessero anche offeso o disprezzato o tenuto in disistima, *giustamente del resto* o mi fossero stati motivo di afflizione - non riconosco che dei fratelli e dei benefattori, a cui sono grato e per cui prego e pregherò sempre.

Nato povero, ma da onorata ed umile gente sono particolarmente lieto di morire povero, avendo distribuito secondo le varie esigenze e circostanze della mia vita semplice e modesta, a servizio dei poveri della Santa Chiesa che mi ha nutrito, quanto mi venne fra mano - in misura assai limitata del resto - durante gli anni del mio sacerdozio e del mio episcopato. Apparenze di agiatezza velarono talora sovente, nascoste a me di affliggente povertà e mi impedirono di dare sempre con la larghezza che avrei voluto. Ringrazio Iddio di questa grazia della povertà di cui fe-

+ Testamentarie qui intese fatta la data del 30 aprile

da Roma - 4 dicembre 1959. Joannes XXIII 1959

Pp.

Pope John's Last Will and Testament

Departing, as I trust, on the road of heaven, I salute and thank and bless the many who so successfully formed my spiritual family—at Bergamo, Rome, in the East, in France, at Venice—and who were my fellow countrymen, benefactors, colleagues, pupils, collaborators, friends, acquaintances; priests, laymen, religious and nuns and those to whom I have been, by the designs of Providence, though unworthily, brother, father and pastor.

The kindness to this poor person from all those I met on the way have made my life serene. I will remember on the threshold of death each and all of those who have preceded me on the last journey, as well as those who will survive and follow me. May they pray for me. I will reciprocate their prayers from purgatory or paradise where I hope to be received, not through my merits, I repeat, but through the mercy of the Lord.

I remember all and I pray for all. But my sons of Venice—the last given to me by the Lord for the final consolation and joy of my priestly life—I wish to name here particularly as a sign of admiration, gratitude and very special tenderness. I embrace them all spiritually, clergy and laity without exception, as I love them without exception as members of the same family, the object of equal paternal and priestly solicitude and affection. "Holy Father, keep them in Thy name those whom Thou hast given Me, that they may be one even as we are" (John 17:11).

In the hour of my farewell, or rather au revoir, I once more point out to all what is most worthy in life: Jesus Christ; the Holy Church; her Gospel; and in the Gospel, above all, the Lord's Prayer (Pater Noster) in the

Mio testamento

Castelgandolfo - 12 sett. 1961

Sotto il respiro caro e confidente di Maria mia Madre celeste, al cui nome è sacra la liturgia di questo giorno, e nell'anno LXXX della mia età, depongo qui e rinnovo il mio testamento, annullando ogni altra dichiarazione circa la mia volontà fatta e scritta precedentemente, a più riprese.

Aspetto e accoglierò semplicemente e lietamente l'arrivo di sorella morte secondo tutte le circostanze con cui piacerà al Signore di inviarmela.

Innanzi tutto chiedo venia al Padre delle misericordie pro innumeris culpis, offensionibus et negligentiis meis come tante e tante volte dissi e ripetei nell'offerta del mio sacrificio quotidiano.

Per questa prima grazia del perdono di Gesù su tutte le mie colpe, e della introduzione dell'anima mia nel beato ed eterno paradiso, mi raccomando alle preghiere e suffragi di quanti mi hanno seguito, conosciuto durante tutta la mia vita di sacerdote, di vescovo, e di umilissimo ed indegno servo dei servi del Signore:

Additions to his will, written in the Pope's own hand.

spirit and heart of Jesus and the Gospel; truth and kindness, a mild and benign kindness, active and patient, invulnerable and victorious.

My children, my brothers, until we meet again! In the name of the Father and of the Son and of the Holy Spirit. In the name of Jesus, our love; of Mary, His and our most tender Mother; of St. Joseph, my first and favorite protector; in the name of SS. Peter, John the Baptist, Mark, Lawrence, Justinian and Pius X. Amen.

In 1957, Pope John added in his own hand:

These pages which have been written by me further attest my absolute will in the case of my sudden death.

Later, in 1961, he added:

Under the dear and confident auspices of Mary, my heavenly mother, to whose name today's liturgy (Sept. 12) is sacred, and in my 80th year, I hereby lay down and renew my testament, canceling all others previously made in written statements on several occasions.

I shall await and receive simply and gladly the arrival of Sister Death according to the circumstances with which the Lord pleases to send her to me.

First and foremost I ask pardon of the Father of Mercy for my numberless sins, offenses and negligences, as I have so often said and repeated in offering my daily Sacrifice of the Mass.

For this gracious pardon of Jesus of all my faults and my entering into the blessed and eternal paradise, I entrust myself to the prayers of all those who have followed me and known me during my lifetime as priest, Bishop and the humblest and most unworthy servant of the servants of the Lord.

I renew integrally and fervently my profession of Catholic, Apostolic and Roman Faith. Among all the various forms and symbols with which the Faith expresses itself, I prefer the priestly and pontifical Creed of the Mass—the most vast and melodious elevation, in union with the Universal Church of every Rite, of every century and of every region, from the "Credo in unum Deum, Patrem omnipotentem" (I believe in one God, the Father Almighty) to the "Et vitam venturi saeculi" (and in the life of the world to come).

THE DAUGHTERS OF ST. PAUL

In Massachusetts
    50 St. Paul's Avenue
    Jamaica Plain,
    Boston 30, Mass.
    172 Tremont St.,
    Boston 11, Mass.
    381 Dorchester St.
    So. Boston 27, Mass.
    325 Main St.
    Fitchburg, Mass.
In New York
    78 Fort Place,
    Staten Island 1, N.Y.
    625 East 187th Street
    Bronx, N.Y.
    39 Erie St.,
    Buffalo 2. N.Y.
In Connecticut
    202 Fairfield Ave.,
    Bridgeport, Conn.
In Ohio
    141 West Rayen Ave.,
    Youngstown 3, Ohio
    Cleveland, Ohio
In Texas
    114 East Main Plaza,
    San Antonio 5, Texas
In California
    1570 Fifth Ave.,
    San Diego 1, Calif.
In Florida
    2700 Biscayne Blvd.
    Miami 37, Florida
In Louisiana
    86 Bolton Ave.,
    Alexandria. La.
In Canada
    8885 Blvd. Lacordaire,
    St. Leonard Deport-Maurice,
    Montreal, Canada
    1063 St. Clair Ave. West,
    Toronto, Canada
In England
    29 Beauchamp Place,
    London, S.W. 3, England
In India
    Water Field Road Extension,
    Plot N. 143,
    Bandra, India
In Philippine Islands
    No. 326 Lipa City,
    Philippine Islands
In Australia
    58 Abbotsford Rd.,
    Homebush N.S.W., Australia